Entrepreneur Mind Hacks

Carey Green

Entrepreneur Mind Hacks

Book 1: Productivity & Creativity

Printed in the United States of America

Copyright © 2014 Carey Green

www.CareyGreen.com

From the Author

You might find this to be a strange book, mainly because it is a compilation of tips from a broad variety of people who live and believe a wide variety of things.

Here's what I mean...

While I am an unapologetic follower of Jesus Christ, many if not most of the contributors to this book are not. At least not that I know of. And that's OK with me.

No matter where you stand on issues of faith I hope neither of those facts causes you to feel uneasy about this book.

My thinking on it is this...

Truth is truth, no matter who speaks it...

...and I'm pleased to present these folks to.

All the contributors to this book have given their time and expertise toward this project for one reason... *we all believe that you have the potential to rock the world.*

Your ideas, your projects, your products, your creative endeavors... all of them can change people's lives and make the world a better place. We hope that our words are able to spur you toward those ends.

As for me personally...

As I said, I'm unapologetic about my faith in Jesus. He's the essence of who I am and my life is entirely His. To deny that or down-play it would be insincere at best and traitorous at worst, so I won't do it. My contributions to this book will reflect that fact. I just want you to know.

If you are a follower of Christ I invite you to connect with me through my personal website & blog. It's my hope that the work the LORD has done in my life can be a tool in His hands to spur you toward what He wants to do in yours.

WHAT'S INSIDE

Let the Mind Hacks Begin

PRODUCTIVITY

There's no magic pill
Carey Green

Quick Tip
David Allen

A calendar-based life
Phyllis Khare

Martin Shervington answers my questions
about Productivity

Tips on staying productive
Dan Crask

Quick Tip
Carey Green

The law of the garden
Carey Green

Tommy Walker answers my questions about
Productivity

Creativity

LET THE
MIND
HACKS
BEGIN...

What this book is and why should you read it.

START HERE...

This is an important book for entrepreneurs

Honestly, it defies categorization. If I were forced to describe it I'd have to say...

- It's a guided self-help book.
- It's short-bursts of life and success coaching... *on steroids.*[1]
- It's a compilation of experiences and perspectives from seasoned and ever-growing business folks.
- It's a seminar on basic business concepts and advanced business mindsets.
- It's a gathering of successful and up-and-coming entrepreneurs involved in a

---

[1] I don't at all mean the "game the system" kind of steroids, but the "mega-success" kind of steroids. Make sense?

free-exchange of ideas, mindsets, and
tactics for life and business.

**My goal in pulling together the people
who have contributed to this book is
three-fold.**

1. I wanted to learn from them.

I admit this first one is a bit selfish.[2]

In my internet wanderings and explorations I
came across all of the contributors you'll find
in this book.

I wanted to learn more from them so I came
up with the idea to invite them to contribute to
a compilation of mind hacks. *I think it was a
pretty good idea.*

2. I want you to learn from them.

It makes sense that if I've received such
benefit from these folks, other people would
too. I want you to be blessed just like I have.

Take these bite-sized portions as an appetizer
of entrepreneurial wisdom. Let it whet your

---

[2] But if you're gonna' learn, you gotta' be selfish to some degree,
right?

taste for more. Let them inspire and motivate you to take action beyond what you're doing now.

You have a lot of good to offer the world - and *only you can give it*. So I encourage you to learn how to maximize that unique gift of yours with the help of the entrepreneurs in this book.

3. I wanted to showcase them.

It's my greatest hope that the contributors to this book benefit from their participation. *So please, visit their websites*, find one or two of them to connect with on a deeper level, and learn, grow, and thrive as a result.

Here's a quick list of the contributors, hyper-linked to their websites. You can find more extensive bios in the back of the book, which are linked to from their individual contributions.

I've listed them in alphabetical order by last name.

Andrea Beltrami, Donnie Bryant, Stephanie Calahan, Julie Coraccio, Susan Finch, Carey Green, Ryan Healy, Phyllis Khare, Jim Kukral, Daniel J. Lewis, Stu McLaren, Tom Morkes,

Katrina Pfannkuch, Tom Rolfson, Martin Shervington, and Tommy Walker.
Book #2 in this series includes these contributors and more.

WHAT YOU'LL FIND HERE

In the pages to follow there's everything from simple quotations to bullet-point lists of tips.

There's essay-type treatments of important mindsets, principles, and how-to's.

There are life-fulfillment suggestions from a variety of perspectives, including spirituality and faith orientations of differing sorts.

There are even Q & A style interviews I did with three of these great folks because they wanted to be involved but didn't have the time to sit down and write something inspiring. So, I suggested a video-chat conversation to be transcribed for this book and they graciously agreed.

You may wonder how so many variations of content can all be considered "Mind Hacks."

It's because every one of them challenges your current thinking.

The reason that's so important is because every productive action begins with a thought, and thoughts originate in the mind.

If you can change your thoughts, you can change your behavior. And if you can change your behavior, you can change your life, or your business, or your family.

It's amazing what a simple beginning life-change can have, isn't it? Thus, I consider everything in this book to be a "Mind Hack."

HOW I COMPILED THIS BOOK

No matter what type of contribution I received from the contributors, the only editing I've done has been for the sake of grammar or comprehension.

And there are a few contributions from different authors that are very similar. I see that as reinforcement that there's truth in what's being said, so I've left those duplicates in the book.
And, who knows: maybe one way a particular concept is said won't hit you, but another way of saying it will. That's my hope.

Having said all of that, I should also say this: I don't agree with everything that's been included this book. I don't suspect you will either.

But I trust that we're all mature enough, wise enough, gracious enough people to accept the opinions and perspectives of others as theirs without feeling that they are pushing their views on us.

As a friend of mine is fond of saying,

Eat the meat and throw away the bones.

APPROACH THIS BOOK WITH HUMILITY

On that note I've got to stop for about a minute to climb up on my soapbox.

Consider this the first mind hack of the book...

It's always been interesting to me that as human beings we can be incredibly open to coaching and help from others when it relates to sports, or music, or education, or business.

For some reason we easily see the value of getting help in those areas.

But when it comes to the more internal, personal issues of life like spirituality, we suddenly get defensive and accusatory *("Don't push your spirituality on me!")*.

There's no other way I can define that except to say that it's **a destructive form of pride.**

It's self-isolation in its worst form. It's cloistering yourself away in a monastic intellectualism that doesn't allow you to consider other alternatives or possibilities that *may* have the potential of informing or helping you.

Not to mention that it's unloving to the people you're unfairly pigeon-holing. I guarantee you, every person is more than the perception you have of what they say.

Imagine if you had an isolationist mindset in your entrepreneurial journey.

- You'd make mistakes you don't have to make.
- You'd go down many wrong roads.
- You'd reinvent the wheel a thousand times over.
- You'd waste tons of time, money, and effort.

Sure, you'd learn a lot of lessons from your mistakes, but they'd be hard-learned lessons you could have learned faster and easier if you'd been humble enough to consider the perspectives of others.

I'm *not* saying that every spiritual perspective has equal value or is equally true, or that you should blindly accept what people say to you about spiritual things.

What I *am* saying is that if you and I have any hope of discovering what really *is* true *in any area*, we've got to be open to considering more than our own limited perspective. I hope you'll do that with this book.

So, some of the contributors to this book (*myself included*) will share things from a spiritual perspective. When you get to those sections there's no reason to become tense or defensive.

Read, consider, and humbly come to your own conclusions.

> ## The truth
> ### is strong enough to hold its
> ### own.

ADDITIONAL RESOURCES

As an added bonus I've included lists of videos and podcast episodes at the end of each section. They lead to talks or interviews that I've found to be especially helpful in one way or another.[3]

Some are from well known people, others not so much. But each of them is a tool you can add to your toolbox to pull out when you need help getting over an obstacle.

---

[3] I'm a podcast freak! They're one of the greatest ways I've been able to ramp up my learning since becoming an entrepreneur!

And if you like the episodes I've included I know the presenters would appreciate it if you checked out the rest of their resources too. So take a stroll over to their site from the links provided.

That's it.

It's time to turn the page and dive in.

One last thing: Be sure you don't only read these short chapters.

Take action.

That's the only way this book can ever bear fruit in your life.

This section is all about
PRODUCTIVITY

There is no magic pill

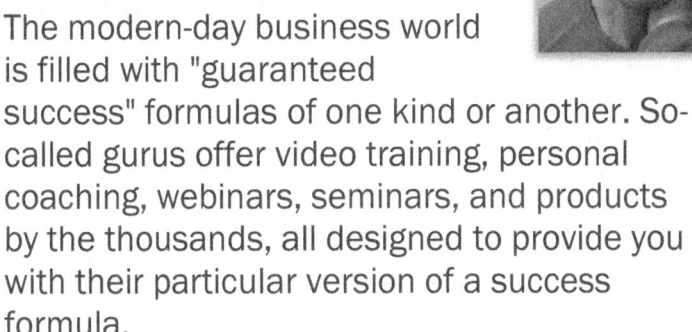

Carey Green

The modern-day business world is filled with "guaranteed success" formulas of one kind or another. So-called gurus offer video training, personal coaching, webinars, seminars, and products by the thousands, all designed to provide you with their particular version of a success formula.

Can those people teach you something helpful? I'm sure many of them can.[4]

But I have little respect for the way many of their programs are marketed. They are hyped, overblown, and made to sound like they will solve every entrepreneurial problem; a one-size-fits-all solution to whatever ails you or your business.

The same types of claims are often made in the realm of time management and productivity. There are numerous systems

---

[4] In reference to the biblical account of Balaam a mentor of mine once said, "If God can speak through a donkey, He can surely speak through that person!"

touted to help you get things done, develop 7 habits to make you highly successful, and on and on.

Again, do these programs have valuable things to offer? Sure. *I even use some of them myself.*

But if you buy into any of those systems thinking they are the equivalent of a magic pill that will solve your disorganization or business vision problems, you're going to be disappointed.

They simply don't work that way.

There is no magic pill.

Embed that last heading in your mind.

No system or methodology, no matter how good, is going to make you an organized or successful person. I urge you to understand that here, at the outset of this book. There's no magic formula that will give you productivity, creativity, relationships, or success.

They simply don't exist.

> **Super productivity, creativity, connections, and true success only come through one thing...**
>
> **YOU**

Don't misunderstand. God Himself is the source of all success that comes your way, but YOU are the conduit through which He brings it. YOU are the means by which it comes.

That means YOU have to put in the effort to see those things come into being. And make no mistake, *it will be the hardest work of your life.*

You will have to undo many years of negative thinking that have held you back.

You'll have to tear down a lifetime of bad habits and replace them with new ones.

And many of you will have to face your deepest fears, murder them in cold blood, and move ahead feeling a freedom you've only dreamed about.

Yes, it's a grisly picture - but a realistic one.

I suggest you spend some time pondering the fact of how difficult it will be to accomplish what you want to accomplish.

Don't just nod your head in acknowledgment.

Don't just agree because it sounds true.

Take the time to consider what it will mean for your life on a practical level.

Things are going to have to change. **You** are going to have to change, and that's the hardest work of all.

Are you ready?

QUICK TIP:

If the task will take 2 minutes or less. Don't procrastinate another second.

DO IT NOW!

Credit for this one goes to

<u>DAVID ALLEN</u>

Living a calendar-based life.

Phyllis Khare

Three years ago my life was a mess.

I was overbooked, overwhelmed and underpaid. I was working late into the night and really had no grip on a long view of where I was going. I had to get my life together and quick or leave all this entrepreneur stuff behind. I started putting everything on my Google calendar - everything. I started creating blocks of time to get stuff done so it wasn't all a wild ride as soon as I turned on the computer.

> ## Amazing things begin to happen when you block out time to get stuff done and
> # STICK TO IT.

I developed some rules and now I have more time, less stress, get so much more done and have free time in my calendar to enjoy my family. If you want to learn more about my relationship with Time explore this post.

http://phylliskhare.com/time-three-years-ago

Martin Shervington answers my questions about productivity

 There are as many ways to think about productivity as there are people. What's your specific definition of productivity?

Getting done what you need to get done by when. Usually, so that other people can get done the things that they need to do when you're part of a team. That's on the high level. I know what projects I have on and being productive is completing each stage of them, and it fits into my model.

My model is strategic, tactical, and operational. Strategy is where everything's going. Then the tactics are the blocks that fit into that, and the operational is doing the work, the blocks that fit into that. That's the sort of model that I run all the time so it's whatever needs to be done in order to achieve that.

 **How do you think about work and the self-discipline that it takes in order to work diligently... I'm asking more about mindset here?**

I think that you've got to have passion. I think if you don't have a passion and you're trying to be productive, it's hard because you're struggling. You're fighting yourself. You don't want to do it. On some level you don't want to do it. Whereas if you've got passion, the vision which goes into strategy, it drives you, it moves you forward and you realize if you don't do the work then you don't get to that next bit.

I wake up pretty much every day 5:30 or 6:00. I get up, first thing I do is turn the computer on, go and make a cup of coffee. and sit down and start. I have systems now that I've really refined that allow me to get through the work quickly in order to get to the next bit of the day. I think that I found a groove on Google Plus and that just allows me to know roughly what the response will be.

There's a crew around now, so I think that when you get to that point and in the first stages, you just do stuff until people start to respond positively towards you and towards it. Once you've got that positivity, it's like actually if I do more of that then people like it and then that allows other things to happen.

Here's an example of a positive. On G+ the other day, a person, "Google hates generalists," and so I put at the top of my share of the post "Be a specialist and Google will love it." I did it and I didn't think about it.

Someone commented on my share and said, "I love the positive spin that you put on it." I didn't realize it but that's very much how I see things. There's no point being negative. Negative tends to get negative.

 **I sometimes hear people say that you don't have to have passion as long as you have a good system and a viable product that people want. But you're saying if you don't have passion you're going to be fighting yourself.**

I can tell from me. I'm not speaking for anybody else on the planet. I'm saying for me, if I didn't have passion it would just be a slog. Because sometimes it really is a slog. particularly if you're working by yourself. It's becoming tough. I know that that's the thing that keeps me going and excited. Even mini projects, I love projects.

I love having a start point and a viewable, vision-able endpoint. Sometimes it may be a month, two months, three months, and then I do that cycle and I get that thing completed. That middle bit you know, it's going to be tough until that last action. It's like you have your ingredients and then you cook it up and then deliver it.

Delivery is more the fun and easy part. The rest of it, you're picking those vegetables or you're growing those vegetables and then you're cooking it. I don't think we'd enjoy the cooking much but the last bit is the fun. I think that is just what I found. Now, do I think people should follow their passion? That's different and I don't think that's necessarily what we should do. I think it's just being passionate if you're going to do something.

Q How do you differentiate between the two?

I've got a passion for surfing. I love surfing. I love windsurfing and all those things. It doesn't mean I should try and become a professional surfer.

Q Not a lot of money in the passion sometimes.

Yeah, but also there are people who are far better and will always be far better both physiologically, attitudinally, all of that, than I will, so even if I've got passion it doesn't mean that that's going to be a good path for me. I think that unless it's very personal and I think that as an entrepreneur, you try stuff out, you fail and sometimes you succeed and you've just got to hope the successes are bigger and more numerous than the nature of the failures.

I think that's something which, Google Plus for me, is a perfect testing ground. Because you can do very low risk things. One post is a test to see people's response, so I think this is why we can do what we can do at "Plus Your Business" and other ventures as well. You can get a crew around you very quickly. You've got to try.

Essentially they go, "Yeah we love that stuff. We'll amplify that. We'll be with you." That helps you to feel more passionate because it's not just you on your own. You then have taken the thing out there and people have gone, "Wow, we like that too." An important element is the supportive groups. You've got just to take things to people and they say, "No, that's unrealistic," or "That isn't quite accurate."

 **Are there any beliefs that you have about yourself personally that you feel make you more productive?**

Right. I'm going to tell you the big secret now because it's probably the best time. It may not come out otherwise. I believe that having an assistant transforms your day when you get to a certain point. This is what I have. I have an assistant that does around between 20 and 40 hours a week.

I do one thing. I create a video of that one thing and that one thing is then able to be rolled out maybe 12 times, 15 times, whatever it might be. It means I can focus on the stuff I'm good at. Let's just say I do a one hour interview. I have one person who transcribes it as it happens and then the transcript comes back. I give it to my assistant. My assistant draws out sections which are quotes and turns it into images with people's faces on it and then the transcript gets put into a PDF document and we have a PDF and we have a standard business format for that.

Then it gets put onto the website and the video gets embedded and it all gets done. That's just me saying, "Hey, can you do this?" It saves me maybe, I don't know, maybe half an hour through quarter an hour for the sake of a minute to two minutes work. I have systems in place that is right across everything I do. just like that. Video production, actual video stuff; instead of me I just use my assistant and that is just amazing, so I'll show her one thing and she saved me two days' work.

Because she could roll out everything, and the instructions are clear and I write little manual things and so on. Maybe it takes 10 minutes, 15 minutes to do that and we have a process. That's it. What do I believe? I believe you don't have to do it all by yourself. You want to find what you're good at and leverage other people's skills if you can.

And I believe friendly wins out. I think that's one thing I think is good. I think optimism wins out. I think people would like to be around people who are being positive and moving forward. I think that's good.

I tend to do that consistently because the alternative is that you get what you give. That's just been my approach .I tend to stay away from anything inflammatory or anything; religion, politics, sex, none of that. You'll see I don't talk about it. It's unimportant in the roles that I'm in.

Offline I'm going to talk about things differently because it's a different amplification but certainly I think that you choose your world. You shape your world by the people that are around you and every conversation that you have.

 Do you have any personal mindsets or beliefs about yourself that you find hard to overcome and if so, how do you overcome those? What do you do mentally to get yourself in a positive place?

I've been, as many people have been, I've had patches when I say I've been depressed. Not for many years but I've had patches in life, certain times and things like that and I think that what happens is the energy goes. There's nothing that you want to wake up for in a way, so your energy goes and you almost implode.

Your senses go inward. Then your mind, your thoughts start to perpetuate negativity and all that. I think that several things help; exercising, eating well. I eat practically no sugar if we're talking about sugar. I don't drink excessively. I just think that you've got to look after yourself and certain times in my life, I probably haven't looked after myself as well as I could have done.

I think it affects you mentally. I think spending time with people who are positive, that's got to be one of the best ways. I think that when I learned a lot of the techniques to run my mind, whether it be from a Buddhist point of view which I've studied for 15 years, or from a new linguistic program point of view which I studied and wrote books on for years, I think that they're useful tools just to be able to understand how we can run our minds.

Basically every thought that we have starts to determine how we behave, so if we are running negative thoughts or anything negative about ourselves, we've got to flip that around because it won't benefit.

Tips on staying productive

Dan Crask

Staying productive is like navigating a minefield of distractions and meaningless work. Sometimes email is a black hole where non-client/non-project "stuff" is grabbing for my attention, and I seem helpless to resist.

Through a lot of trial and error (heavy on the error) I have a few mind hacks to keep me productive:

Mandatory Door

For the past 7 years I have worked from a home office most of the time. I began full time self-employment when my oldest son was only two months old, and we now have three children. I place a very high value on being present and available to my kids, yet I am also responsible for earning the money for our family. It is nothing short of God's grace that none of my kids know what it's like for their mom or dad to "leave for work."

The downside to this, though, is that I am always available to the point where, once my oldest could crawl, I knew I needed my office to be in a room with a door.

Simply having a door that can close, and maybe even lock, is key for me to stay productive. When the door is closed the kids know to be quiet and don't bother me.

Notifications Serve Me (not the other way around)

One of the best decisions I've made as a professional is to turn all notifications off, save for texts, calls, and reminders. My phone, tablet, and computer have no badges, no tones, nothing. When I want to know if I have an email, I go to email and see. If I want to know if my post was shared or commented on Google Plus, I won't know until I open it up later in the day.

NO notifications.

I find that notifications, while intended for productivity, are nothing but shiny objects, robbing well-meaning people of staying on task. I am not impressed by multi-taskers. I am, however, impressed by the professional who keeps "maker's hours" to hone his/her concentration on a single task for hours, producing excellence.

Start Early

This is a recent one. I find that by starting work within 30 minutes of waking up, I can crank out more work in the first 4 hours of the day than I could if I got started at 10:00 am.

QUICK TIP:

Daily Reset

Every day, without fail, spend the first 20 to 30 minutes of the day resetting your thinking - about yourself, your goals, and your daily projects.

DO NOT start your day without **ABSOLUTE CLARITY**

regarding your most important tasks for the day.

Those 20 minutes will determine the tone, course, and productivity of your entire day.

Carey Green

The law of the garden

Carey Green

When I first married, I was a block-head of a kid who didn't know even *half* of what I'm writing in this book.

To illustrate how bad it was, my lovely bride, after only a month or two of being married to me, began to call me a "floater."

What's a floater?[5]

A floater is a person who floats... from one event or circumstance to another with little real thought about his place or responsibility in those events. Things just "happen" to a floater and a floater just floats through it.

Whatever *it* is.

When Mindi first labeled me a "floater," I took offense.

---

[5] No, it's not those things in your drink after your 3 year old shares the glass with you... though it's pretty close.

"I'm not a floater," I argued.

But the more she explained what she meant, the more I understood.

There were things I wanted to accomplish, goals of a sort. But I hadn't realized that if I wasn't actively taking steps to achieve those goals, they probably weren't going to happen.

In short...

I hadn't given much thought to the fact that I was responsible for my life.

I know, I know... that's really dumb. But like I said, I was a block-head of a kid.

Organizing your life may be the most important thing you ever do.

Why would I say that?

Because it's true.

You, just like me, will be a floater if you don't do something to prevent it. It's a principle I've come to call **"The Law of the Garden."**

Here's how it works:

You can't plant a garden, neatly in rows, and expect it to produce all on its own. You have to do some work to keep it in an optimal growth state.

You have to water it, weed it, and fertilize it. In many cases, you have to remove excess fruit, veggies, or branches (*called pruning*) so that the plants can produce even better fruit in the future.

The point of this principle is that if you don't do something to organize or order your life, it's going to naturally move toward disorganization all on its own.

Like an untended garden your life will be overrun by weeds (*laziness, apathy, lack of direction, pettiness, etc.*). You'll become a floater... and your life will yield the produce of a floater, which honestly, isn't much.

I care about you.

I care enough to warn you: Your life's purpose is in danger of being missed if you don't wake up to your responsibility for it. You are in danger of frittered away the most valuable gift God has given you - your life.

I don't want you to be one of the multitudes who wake up in their old age and realize that they didn't do anything worthwhile with their lives.

I want your life to count.

It's said that Abraham Lincoln once quipped,

"The average man dies at 19 and is buried at 75."

Abe is saying that most people let any spark of ambition they might have had as a child, fizzle away by the time they are grown.

They spend the rest of their lives just waiting to die.

That, my friends, is being a floater. That is wasting your life.

It doesn't have to happen to you.

Tommy Walker answers my questions about productivity

 There are likely as many ways to think about productivity as there are people. How do YOU define productivity for yourself?

Productivity for me is about making sure I complete the things I say I'm going to complete.

Obviously, this doesn't always happen. However, I try to be honest with myself and have tried to adopt Seth Godin's "Thrash Early" concept, which is about doing all of my own mental fits early on as to whether a project is even something I want to commit to.

From there, I have to be honest with myself and remember that I'm probably going to forget if it's not something that's not immediately pressing for my survival.

If it involves other people, I will let them know up front that I am interested and may need frequent reminders in order to take something over the finish line, but I am interested in completing the project and will dedicate the time for it.

On the flip side, I don't commit to projects that don't interest me, this minimizing my own drudge work, and keeping me focused on the projects I really want to complete and put my stamp on.

 **How do you think about work and the self-discipline it takes to work diligently?**

I think it's important that you stay honest with yourself about the kind of work you want to put your name on, and the kind of impression you want that work to make.

Too often, we take on work we're not passionate about on some level, which translates to not being as diligent in completing the macro and micro tasks necessary to complete the project.

If you're focusing on doing the stuff you're passionate about, than I think the diligence will follow.

But, I'd be remiss to imply that *all* work is passionate work. Far from it. There are plenty of "little things" that are involved with any project that make you want to bang your head on the desk and will make your eyeballs melt out of their sockets if you have to look at it any longer.

When that's the case, I just force myself to finish what's necessary and keep going.

Also, it's important to have deadlines and that you ship by those deadlines. Not everything has to be perfect, and God knows I've shipped half-perfect things for the sake of meeting deadline (note: there is a difference between half-perfect & mediocre. Never ship mediocre).

As long as the goal is about making sure your low bar is still higher than the other guy's high bar, you'll be ok.

Give me your top 3 reasons productivity is important to you.

1. If you can't ship, nobody else will no what you're capable of.

2. If you don't have some organizational structure for yourself, you'll constantly be fighting against yourself to actually ship

3. Lack of productivity leads to stagnation, stagnation leads to apathy, and apathy crushes momentum faster than anything.

Are there any beliefs you have about yourself that make you more productive?

Not a belief so much as a practice.

My wife recommended to me that I create a file system on my computer that allows me to keep all of my blog drafts, images, and research organized.

An example of how I might get to a specific article from last year would look like this:

Clients -> ConversionXL -> 2013 - November - Why Simple Websites Are Scientifically Better

In this folder are all of the images used in the article along with additional folders that contain all of the outgoing links I used in the article, and a contact sheet for all of the admins of the authors of the pieces I've linked out to.

This allows me to create a contact database that makes distribution a little easier and systematic further down the road.

 **Are there any beliefs you have about yourself that make you less productive?**

Not really... however I do need to outsource and delegate more. That's my pursuit moving forward.

However, it used to be that I would write when I "felt like it" or was "inspired" and while that would certainly be nice, it's unrealistic as my income ultimately depends on the words that flow from my head to my fingers. It was only when I stopped being precious about everything and started getting it done and working with my editors when I needed help that everything started taking off for me.

 **What do you do to fight or minimize those beliefs?**

I'm not afraid to ask for help. Seriously.

There have been pieces I've written where I'd show it to another writer or my editor and be like "I'm totally stuck, can you help me find where it's not working and help me with the direction on this piece?"

Even though I'm considered an "expert" I firmly believe that nobody is an island, and it's

important to suck up any pride you might have and admit when you need
help, *especially* when you do creative work.

One question that can move you forward with amazing speed

Stephanie Calahan

I work with purpose-driven solo entrepreneurs and small business owners who are really amazing at what they do. They have achieved great success in their business but may have done so at the expense of their personal freedom, or well-being and happiness. That makes them feel over-worked and out of balance. Many times it causes them to be limited in terms of growth because their business lacks scalability.

When I think of those scenarios, the visual I always seem to come back to is a hamster wheel. I remember watching my brother's hamsters when I was young. They would run and run in that wheel, but could not get traction to move anywhere. Some would run so hard that they'd fall asleep in the wheel!

As I meet people, I see some of *them* in wheels too.

They are hard workers and they are smart, but they are in a wheel and many of them don't even recognize it.

Some have even found their way out of the wheel and moved forward to create great success in their business, only to learn that they created a bigger *wheel*!

They find themselves in a painful place because the success that they've created has come back to hurt them. They spend way more time in their business than they want to. They do things they may not want to do in the name of success and they find their business is running them rather than them running their business.

They've lost the freedom they were seeking when they became an Entrepreneur.

The saddest thing is that when they get sucked into working this way, they often find they are lacking in other things.

They may find that relationships start to crumble or they feel guilt for not participating in other areas of life.

Even worse, their health could be affected; that was what happened to me.

I was already doing it to myself over and over in my corporate life and when I started my own business I found myself doing it again because I'm a super-achiever-go-getter. I'm really great at what I do, but I got sucked in and let the business take over me and my life; and I nearly died.

I know that is an extreme statement, but I was literally given a year to live if I didn't turn around my manner of living and being. **I had created a bigger wheel.**

In today's "guru"-led business world, it is easy to get caught up in "should-dos." It is easy to add a million things to your to-do list.

One of the guiding questions that I focus on and teach my clients is this:

"Is what I'm doing guiding me to my ultimate freedom or am I running back to that hamster wheel or worse, making a bigger wheel?"

Now I'm on a mission: to teach as many entrepreneurs as I can to recognize where they are, to be okay with that, and put strategies and systems into their life so that they don't have to experience the pain of success, but they can experience real freedom, ultimate freedom in their life. What would that mean to you? How would you define ultimate/real freedom in your business and life?

Do you find that you relate to that story; your business is not giving you the freedom that you really desire?

The basic concept is that many entrepreneurs find themselves running in a "hamster wheel" where they are working hard, but not really going where they want at the speed they want. If you find this analogy familiar, here is what you can do:

Ultimate Freedom in Six Steps

Step 1 - Recognize that you are "in the wheel" and say "Enough With the Craziness!" Decide to alter your path.

Step 2 - Slow the wheel down for a short while so you can evaluate the strategy and effectiveness of what you are doing.

Step 3 - Acknowledge how far you have come! For many people, when they realize they are "in the wheel", they start to self criticize or beat themselves up. Try not to do that.

Step 4 - Figure out how the "wheel" was created.

Step 5 - Figure out what you want instead.

Step 6 - Put the mindset, strategy, systems, and automation in place to make that vision happen.

Ultimate Freedom in six steps.

Yes, it can take time to do these steps, but the value you get in return is priceless.

QUICK TIP:

Not everyone needs to be easily reached by e-mail.

Some people, such as those who deal with clients all day or manage large teams that crave frequent guidance, should be pros at this skill.

But other people, like computer programmers, writers, advertising gurus, and professors, should be free to suck at e-mail just as much as they might suck at other skills that aren't that relevant to their core value proposition.

This one comes from **Cal Newport**

Embrace your cycles

Julie Coraccio

I am a recovering Type A personality. Being a Type A personality is not all bad; I couldn't have accomplished what I have without my organizational skills and my ability to stay on top of it all.

As I have gotten older, I have found I can be more productive by tweaking how I do things and honoring different aspects of myself.

I like to call it a detached productivity.

Embrace Your Cycles

We live in the real world, so for the majority of us, we cannot sit around going with the flow 24/7. And we're not supposed to.

Flow is feminine; taking action is male. It's about balancing and listening for when you need to take action and when you need to sit back and let it unfold.

For example, Imagine that someone contacted you about hiring you for your services. Once you sent your bid, discussed your services, etc., would you wait for a response or would you continue to call to see if they were going to hire you? You most likely would say, "I have done all I can do and need to wait to see what happens."

That is flow.

I am writing the first draft of this article in bed. I had the flu for two days last week, rested, got better, and a few days later caught a cold.

In the past I used to fight being sick. I would continue to exercise, ignore my body and go a million miles a minute. As a result, I would end up being ill for longer.

That was one of the earliest ways I learned to go with the flow. I don't fight or try to change the situation; I listen and accept.

Exercise:
- Practice sitting quietly and listening to yourself.

- What does your body need? Your mind? Your emotions? Your spirit?
- Honor whatever you need to and focus on that.
- Don't worry about your to do list; focus on what you need to give attention to at this time.
- Trust you will know when it is time to get back to work.

The power of organization

Carey Green

I mentioned my wife earlier. Her name is Mindi. She's one of God's greatest blessings in my life.

Mindi is a professional homemaker and mom.

By "professional" I mean that she literally *makes* our home a home. You know what I'm saying? I wish she could get paid for it.[6]

The excellence with which she does her job (*physically, relationally, emotionally*) rivals that of any high-producing company today.

Move over Google.

How does she do it? *Through organization.*

For as long as I've known Mindi, she's been a list-maker. She keeps track of the needs and responsibilities that fall within her realm. And

---

[6] Yes, I know. Living with me should be payment enough. That's what you were thinking, right?

there are a *lot* of needs and responsibilities within her realm.

She puts together a plan to ensure that everything gets done. She's even been known to finish a task that wasn't on her list, then write it on her list just so she can cross it off! (*If you're laughing, it's probably because you do the same thing.*)

The outcome of Mindi's organization is a well-ordered home that blesses everyone in the family and the people who come to visit. It's an example of one of the many benefits that organization can provide.

Here are some of the benefits of a well-ordered life:

- Balance

When you're organized no one thing will take over your schedule or monopolize your time. You deal with your responsibilities and relationships on purpose.

- Peace

Organization enables you to have confidence that the important things in life are the things you're actually doing. On the flip side, you'll know that everything that is truly important has a place in your plan and will get done.

- Focus

An outgrowth of having tasks and projects organized is that your mind will be free to focus on one thing at a time because everything else has its allotted time to be done later.

- Value

An organized life enables you to see what is truly important and how you can do your part to see it come about.

You'll know that your life is taking on great significance as you live in an orderly, purposeful way.

No more feeling like your day was wasted.

No more wondering if you accomplished anything of lasting purpose.

Organization helps you ensure that your life is adding up to something meaningful.

QUICK TIP:

"If you don't marry an impulse with an action in

LESS THAN 5 SECONDS

you'll pull the emergency brake and kill the idea.

Your problem isn't ideas, your problem is you don't act on them."

This beauty comes from

MEL ROBBINS

Daily and master to-do lists

Andrea Beltrami

If you're anything like me you swear by your to-do list, and for good reason.

It's a great way to stay on track and get the most out of your time. But they can also be overwhelming, psyching us out before we even get started. It's easy to get stuck because we're focusing on the whole picture instead of the first step. It's human nature.

> I've found that by organizing my to-do list into two separate lists - a **MASTER LIST** and a **DAILY LIST** - I get the best of both worlds.

Here's How I Do It

At the beginning of each year and again at the beginning of each new quarter, I sit down and write a master list of tasks, projects and things I want/need to accomplish over the next 3 months.

Then at the end of each work day I open my master list, I cross off any tasks I completed and I create the next days to do list.

It's crucial to keep your daily to do list realistic and achievable and not commit to too much. That's setting yourself up for failure.

Don't go broad, keep it narrow and specific.

I'd suggest 2-3 things that you have to accomplish that day (*something you need to write or create, calls you need to make, any projects you need to outline, research that needs to be done, etc*) and another 2-3 small things (*errands or things you need to do around the house, etc*) that you'd like to do but that aren't critical.

Often those smaller tasks get carried over to the next day's list (*sometimes for days*) and that's ok. It's more important that you tackle the 2-3 critical items.

Those are the things that will bring you closer to whatever the current goal is you're trying to attain.

Two simple tricks for focus and time management

Daniel J. Lewis

Trick #1: Schedule your tasks.

This seems obvious, but most people don't do it.

- If you need time to process your email, schedule it.
- If you want to regularly create blog, podcast, or YouTube content, schedule it.
- If you want to answer questions on social media, schedule it.

This approach has helped me be consistent with my blogging and conquer my email inbox.

Trick #2: Use a timer to avoid distractions.

Often, we can't accomplish much in a day because we're getting distracted. An email came in, a tweet, a call, something funny, and more.

- When you are trying to focus on something, start a timer for 25 minutes and work on nothing else but that one task.
- When you want to chase a distraction, remind yourself that you're free to do that when your timer is finished.
- After the 25 minutes, you can take a 5-minute break to chase the distractions.
- But if you're in "the zone" of good momentum, just reset the timer for another 25 minutes.
- Use your smart phone or www.e.ggtimer.com for easy timer creation.

Tom Rolfson

answers my questions about productivity.

Q   **Tom, how do you define productivity for you?**

How do I define productivity? OK, that's a fair question, a good question. I guess a productive day is staying on task and on point for my primary purpose, while still allowing myself flexibility or creativity time. You know, the ability to grow with an idea or grow an idea is really important and key to my productivity.

Q   **So that requires a certain amount of self-discipline?**

Yeah, very much so. If it's an administrative task, I have to be very stringent with my schedule. And in doing that, that involves also eliminating all the distractions. That means no Google+, no Twitter, no social media of any kind. Sometimes literally shutting the phone off to all distractions for a couple hour period at a time.

But with the creative stuff, the problem with that is keeping it from interfering with the other more finite tasks. I love scheduling periods of two, three, four hours to work on exploring an idea or set of ideas whether it's related to developing a storyboard for a video or exploring the direction of the development of a website might go.

 **Are there any beliefs that you have about yourself personally that you feel make you more productive?**

OK. Well I started my first corporation at 16 years old. Probably from my late teens, my early 20s, I conquered the philosophy of not taking on a project unless I found some real fulfillment in it. I mean fulfillment either in the realm of entertainment, which means fulfillment with the creativity involved, or the product itself. Or a personal sense of fulfillment with regards to the project itself being one where I can see a direct benefit for other people. It doesn't always have to be a tangible or measurable thing.

For example: my involvement with a non-profit, developing ways to track online predators or pedophiles. It's pretty difficult to measure what kind of success you have with that. But still, something like that I find really rewarding. And I don't consider it work. It's not work when you are doing something like that.

So what I'm saying is that there has to be some kind of personal satisfaction with my effort. Where is my effort going? If I can see that and in some measurable or quantifiable way see it, that's what matters. So number one, I guess, is simply that there needs to be some kind of personal satisfaction I get from it.

Number two is... I guess I would be remiss if I didn't mention some kind of fiscal or monetary gain. I love to help other people but I believe that I operate by a philosophy that if I'm doing something to help somebody else profit or prosper, I should, in turn, be rewarded in that capacity

And number three is just simply learning. Being able to learn with every challenge, every task. In the process of being productive, I'm going to expand my capabilities.

One of the things that I firmly believe about myself is that I'm not... How do I put it... an extraordinary person. I was given an extraordinary *opportunity* when my dad taught me computer design at the age of 12. He didn't just teach me ones and zeros and how to manipulate ones and zeros. He taught me how to take my technical knowledge of how a computer performs and look at a real world situation and find a way to make it more productive, more profitable, easier or more widely available to many people. And so, a belief about myself is, well, a lot of people have called me a visionary or things like that because of my role in online development. I just feel I was a guy given the opportunity to be in the right place at the right time.

 **Do you have or have you had any limiting beliefs about yourself that have hampered your productivity?**

Yes, there have been times where I've had limiting beliefs and difficulties because of the path that I've chosen. For example, quitting school at 16 years old to start a corporation. I went on to get a technical college degree and I started some formal university but I quit because I had too great an opportunity.

So there have been times when I've said, "I can't do that because I don't have a PhD." But I've been able to turn form that and so when I look at an obstacle, I say, "If this can be accomplished, why can't I do it?"

Sacrifice wisely

Carey Green

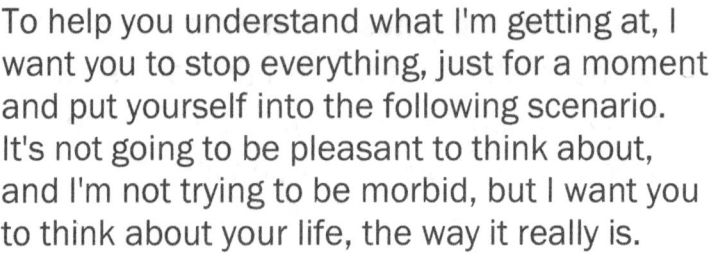

In order to be super productive there are many things you'll have to sacrifice[7]. But there are a few things you should never, *never* sacrifice for the sake of productivity.

To help you understand what I'm getting at, I want you to stop everything, just for a moment and put yourself into the following scenario. It's not going to be pleasant to think about, and I'm not trying to be morbid, but I want you to think about your life, the way it really is.

OK, here comes the imaginary scenario. *Are you ready?*

You're dying of cancer.

You're in the hospital, connected to more wires and tubes than you can imagine. Surrounding you are your family members, some friends, and a bevy of doctors and nurses who are trying to figure out how to tell

---

[7] Sacrifice is the essence of love. If it doesn't cost you something to help someone, what is it really worth?

you that you only have a month remaining of your earthly existence.

You begin to look back on the life you've lived. You begin to wonder what your life will count for once you're gone.

OK, come back to the present.

Why did I make you imagine such a horrid thing? *Because it's going to happen to you.*

It might not be cancer but you WILL face the end of your life some day.

You might approach it slowly through the process of aging. You might approach it quickly as you see the lights of a MACK truck bearing down on your windshield. Either way, you're going to die.

When that day comes, what will matter most to you?

One thing I can tell you for certain about that day, is this: *the things that matter most to you then will not be things, they will be people.*

I know. I served as a Pastor for over 20 years. I saw person after person approach death and their thoughts were not on their cars, bank accounts, or career achievements.

They were thinking about the people they were leaving behind.

Sometimes that concern manifested itself in regrets ("*I wish I'd cared for my family differently.*"). Other times it came out in gratitude ("*I'm so blessed to have had the family and friends I did.*").

When that day comes for you, which way do you want your thoughts to go?

If you sacrifice the relationships in your life for the sake of productivity or success, that day will be one of regret for you. It's not worth getting super organized and crazily productive if it costs you relationships.

Do you hear what I'm saying?

PEOPLE are more important than things.

They are, really.

Your possessions, accomplishments, and bank accounts will not endure beyond this earth. *But people will.*

You've been given a limited number of vital relationships in your life. You need to manage them well as you navigate your entrepreneurial career. Those people need your love and attention; they need your care. They need you to be as intentional about your interactions and concern for them as you are about any important business transaction or creative project.

In fact, they need it more.

Getting organized and becoming productive will require sacrifice, but make sure the things you sacrifice are things, not people.

It's a good thing to want to be productive. But, it's another thing to want to be productive to the exclusion of things that are more important than being productive.

That's called messed-up-priorities and it's something I'm going to delve into in my next chapter.

QUICK TIP:

Activity without

PURPOSE

is the

DRAIN

of your life.

Wisdom from

Tony Robbins

Measure it!

Ryan Healy

Whatever you measure improves.

Therefore, you need to identify key metrics in your business that you can measure.

Simply by measuring key numbers, your subconscious mind will go to work to try to improve them.

You can take it to the next level by reviewing your key metrics daily, weekly, or monthly and actively working to improve them.

My friend Stephen Dean once wrote that the best productivity method is the new one. This really resonated with me. And if you think about it, I think you'll find it's true.

It's easy to get excited about a new productivity technique and be faithful to it for a month or two. But over time it can become tedious. The strategy or technique may lose some its motivational power.

Therefore, you may consider focusing on one key metric in Month #1, a different key metric in Month #2, and another key metric in Month #3. By doing this, you maintain some of the natural excitement that comes with doing anything new.

Obviously, you may want to continue measuring *all* your key metrics every month (*to make sure your business isn't slipping*), but focus on improving just one metric each month.

This keeps things fresh and interesting and helps prevent burnout.

Clutter: let it go, let it go, let it go

Julie Coraccio

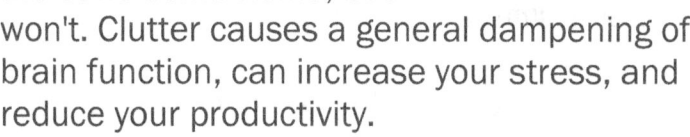

I can bore you with stats till the cows come home, but I won't. Clutter causes a general dampening of brain function, can increase your stress, and reduce your productivity.

Letting go of clutter helps you create the life you want. Feng Shui experts say that this is the first thing that needs to happen before doing any Feng Shui.

The point is, you can reduce clutter to increase your productivity.

A tip I share with people who do multiple projects is to use a literature sorter. You can keep items for a project in one single cubbie; with lots of cubbies you can keep together lots of projects.

Exercise:

- Tackle an area of your house or office that has a clutter problem.

- If it is tough, start with 5 minutes a day. Put on a timer if need be and schedule it in your planner.
- As you start to let go of clutter on the outside, it also helps with clutter on the outside.

Or start with inner clutter:

- Are you your biggest cheerleader or your worst enemy?
- Is there a project you need to let go of to move on to bigger and better things?

Discover your "big rocks" <u>Carey Green</u>

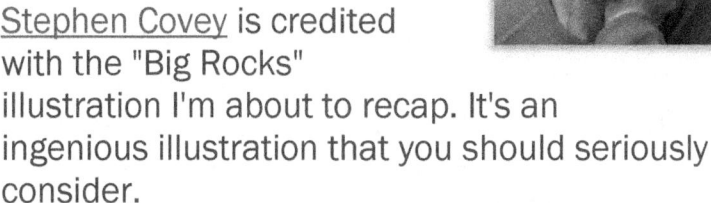

<u>Stephen Covey</u> is credited with the "Big Rocks" illustration I'm about to recap. It's an ingenious illustration that you should seriously consider.

Stephen takes a large glass jar and fills it with colored gravel. He likens all those tiny little rocks to the varied things that press into our lives to take up our time and energy.

Next, Stephen gives a participant a lot of other, *bigger* rocks. Each is labeled to represent things that need to be a part of a healthy life.

- Family
- Faith
- Friends
- Work responsibilities
- Great opportunities
- Vacation
- And the list goes on

He tells the participant that she has to get all the rocks into the jar with nothing sticking out at the top.

Inevitably, she can't do it.

She can't do it until Stephen tells her she can use a different paradigm to get the job done. That's when the participant puts the rocks into an empty jar and pours the tiny rocks in around them.

What she discovered is that the big rocks have to go in first.[8]

The big rocks represent what is

MOST IMPORTANT.

They are critical things that must be done or else very negative, even disastrous results may happen.

---

[8] If you've never seen this great illustration in action you can watch it on YouTube here.

You need to discover your "big rocks."

Have you taken the time to consider what things absolutely must go into your typical day?

More importantly, have you considered what the most important things are that should fit into your life?

Most people haven't. Most people float through life wondering why it's moving so fast and why the truly important things seem to always get squeezed out. They haven't taken the time to thoughtfully consider what their personal, most important, non-negotiable, must-be-in-my-life priorities are.

Make your own "big rocks" list

Right now, I want you to get out a piece of paper and brainstorm your own "big rocks" list.

Think through all the areas of your life. Once you have the list written out, go get something to drink and come back to it. The time away will allow you to think of a few more things that need to be on your list. When your list is done, order it according to importance, with the most important things at the top. Do you have it? Good.

The list you've made represents the most vital things to you, personally. They are the things that if left undone or neglected will cause the most destruction, harm, or grief to you. Because the things on that list are so important, you've got to make sure that you get those things into your everyday life, first.

Why first?

The things on your list have to be inserted into your life and schedule first because your life is like Stephen Covey's jar. Many small things will work their way into your schedule over time, demanding your attention and consuming your energy to the point that the most important priorities won't fit into your routine no matter how hard you try.

But that will only happen if you let it.

How do you prevent it from happening? You build a simple but powerful thing for yourself called a system.

> **When you develop a system that puts your big rock priorities into your life and workflow FIRST, it's almost like**
>
> # MAGIC!

But it's not magic; it's the way God designed the world to work. Here's what I mean:

Creation itself is made up of various systems:
- The solar system
- The water cycle
- The human body

These and thousands of other things in the known universe operate according to set patterns and predictable rules we call "laws of nature." Like clockwork they do what they do without fail, producing amazing results like sunrises, thunderstorms, and heartbeats.

The very same system-principle that makes the created order *keep* its order and produce its wonders can be applied to the way you live your life.

A finely tuned, well thought-out system will enable you to get more things done in a day than you ever thought possible, and amazingly, you'll feel more productive too. That's because you are getting the most important things done first.

As a result, your mind will be free of the burden of responsibility that "big rocks" automatically carry with them.

That's when you'll have the mental energy to focus on other important things, creative things, relational things, things that can move you toward even greater success.

Systems are powerful.

They're the subject of my next contribution to this book.

ONE LAST THING: Your "big rocks" will vary, depending on your life.

If two people, say a brain surgeon and a plumber, sat down at the same table to write out their individual "big rocks" lists, they'd come up with two very different lists, wouldn't they?

Of course they would.

That's because each of them has responsibilities and circumstances that are different from the other guy. As a result, their lists have to be different.

But there would be quite a few things on their lists that are exactly the same, don't you think?

Things like family, work, physical fitness, spiritual health, etc. These are the things that require deliberate attention and focus. They are also the things that have to go into the life-jar first.

So go ahead. Write out the big rocks list that fits your life and family.

Do it.

QUICK TIP:

God will not allow any person to keep you from your destiny.

They may be bigger, stronger, smarter, and more powerful, but **GOD** knows how to get you where you're supposed to be.

A treasure from our old friend

Anonymous

An iPhone voice memo app that just works

Stu McLaren

If you've ever had an idea (*and weren't at your computer*), then you'll love this new 3-step process I've created for capturing my ideas while on the go.

I decided to create this process after my drive to the airport. While in my car I began listening to some podcasts and inevitably, I had some ideas. The problem was, I didn't have an easy way to capture them.
Sound familiar?

Until I developed this new process, my options were:

A) **Try to text or email the idea to someone while driving** – which obviously isn't safe.

B) **Try to record a voice memo** – which turning into a text document afterwards required a whole bunch of other steps (*and therefore didn't happen*).

C) Try to "remember" the idea for later when I was near a computer – and you know that never worked.

Once I got to the airport, I had a little time before my flight so I decided to finally figure this out.

With the help of a recording app, a web service and my assistant, I now have a super simple 3-step process that virtually guarantees my ideas are captured.

What's even better is that when I need to reference these voice memos, I have an audio version, a text version and they are searchable as soon as I get back to my computer.
Here's how to replicate this process:

Step #1 - Setup a Dropbox Account

DropBox is a web based service that I use every day to store and share files. I've tried many others like Box.com and Google Drive but the reason I continue to stick with Dropbox is because it's so darn easy to integrate into other areas of my business.

It's free to setup a basic account which gets you up to 2GB of storage but I upgraded to their Pro account for $10/month because I use it a lot and needed more storage (*which is still a bargain*).

So for this "Voice Memo" process, you'll need a Dropbox account and the free plan will definitely be enough storage to get you started.

Step #2 - Download the DropVox App (works with iPhone and iPad)

The "secret sauce" of this process is the app called <u>DropVox</u>.

There are many apps for recording your voice but this one keeps things ultra simple and does exactly what I needed it to do.

It has one button – record. Then, it automatically uploads the recording to your Dropbox account and puts the audio file in whatever folder you want – I put mine in a folder called "DropVox" (*you only have to select this folder the first time you use the app*).

Pretty straight forward right?

Then all you need to do is "share" the Dropbox folder with your assistant, ask them to check it each day for new recordings and transcribe the files (*they can find the latest files by clicking the "Modified" link to sort the files by recent activity*).

TIP: When I record an idea, I try to first record the title of the voice memo, then leave a 2-3 second pause. Then I record the idea. That way my assistant knows that I'd like the title of the memo to be.

Step #3 – Add The Transcription To Evernote

For some people, this step may not be necessary because you could easily add the transcribed files to the same Dropbox folder (*which I also do as a backup*) or even just have them emailed to you.

However, Evernote has become my digital brain and it's the tool I use to organize my ideas. So because of that, I wanted the transcriptions also added to my account so that I could easily search/find them (*or any content within each transcription*).

One other thing I would suggest is to ask your assistant to also list the Dropbox link to the original recording at the bottom of each transcription. That way if you ever need to listen to the original recording again, you can easily find it.

TIP: Have your assistant also tag each voice memo transcription with a specific tag in Evernote just in case you have trouble finding it through the regular search (*my tag is "transcription"*).

Now when I'm driving, I just make sure I have the DropVox app open. Then when I'm hit with a flash of brilliance (*smile*), I just press record knowing that the ideas will be ready for me the next time I need them.

Building a business is hard enough but I'm finding the more time I take to create these types of processes, the more efficient I become.

Your Turn

Do you have a process or "hack" that helps you be more efficient?

4 simple ways to live your passion every day

Katrina Pfannkuch

Living your passion is a feeling that expands beyond the container of words we have to explain it.

It's an inner knowing that's desired yet sometimes also feared, and it drives you to follow the path it carves until you feel it's energy flow through you effortlessly.

With something so powerful within us, why aren't we actively expressing our passion every day?

We aren't always sure how to mix it into to a busy life.

There are some things you can do to tap into your true desires and practice building up the inner "pipeline" to express passion in all you do. Pulling in your natural creative side throughout the day is a lot easier when you've made room for it to flow through all moments, not just the moments you set aside to actively "create".

To help make room for more creative passion in your life, here are some ways to make it a priority.

1. **Wake up early enough to savor "one thing" in solitude before you start the day.**

Some people naturally like to wake up early. I am not one of those people. However, I have come to recognize the value of honoring a regular morning routine before rushing into a full day. I also know how off balance I feel when I miss my "one thing".

Some examples include:
- a cup of coffee in peace and quiet
- a morning run
- a few yoga poses
- or a simple meditation

It can be whatever gives you a sense of balance when you start the day. Just stick to it!

2. **Choose a skill, aptitude or talent about yourself, and express gratitude for it.**

It's easy to focus on what you don't know or have yet, but what about what you do have?

Why not spend time and energy connecting with how it feels to be good at something, how it feels to be connected to your natural gifts?

Even if they may not seem significant to you, the things you are good at absolutely count as part of your passion expression. When you can acknowledge and honor what you already do well, it reminds you of how it feels to be in the flow, led by your passion.

3. **Naturally slip your passion into daily exchanges with others.**

To make the most of each moment you have with a person, share an aspect of your passion within the exchange.

Tell a story, offer support or a tip, express gratitude, give a compliment, or simply say hello in a way that's unique to you.

Not only will you feel good about expressing an aspect of yourself in a way that feels natural, but the extra practice will help you feel more comfortable.

For example, I love being able to help people see their true beauty and gifts. To share a bit of my passion in a personal exchange, I offer a compliment. This allows me to express my gift while also helping another person see their own beauty reflected back to them. Who knows what kind of impact that will have on their day?

4. Read Something Inspiring

Sometimes one little sentence can turn your day completely around.

Reading a poem, mantra, book passage or article that helps you block out the world and re-center focus on your passion can be the little boost you need to remember what drives you to pursue something you love.

Jim Kukral
answers my questions about productivity

 My thinking is that there's likely as many ways to think about productivity as there are people. I'm curious how you define productivity for yourself.

I'm a little bit different than other people where I don't have specific stuff that I have to get done every single day and that's one of the poor things. Give me the question again.

 Sure. How do you define productivity for yourself?

How do I define productivity for myself? It's reaching certain goals that I set for myself based upon larger vision of the business that I'm trying to run. I work it backwards. I wrote a book called Business Around a Lifestyle.

The whole concept of this is that I first decide what I want my lifestyle to be then I work backwards to build the businesses that I need to have so that I can have that lifestyle. For example, I decide that I really don't like working forty hour weeks. I like to take time off. I like to go fishing and I like to spend time coaching my kid's football and softball and volleyball and baseball teams and be at every event.

I have designed a lifestyle that I want and built a business around it so that I guess you tie this whole thing into productivity is that I only do the work that I need to do to reach that lifestyle. It drives me because if I want to maintain that lifestyle I've got to be able to be productive based upon the things that I need to do. It's kind of a roundabout way saying that that's how I handle it. The lifestyle motivates me to be productive when I need to be is I guess my shorter way of saying it.

 **So, you pick the lifestyle you want. You determine what it takes to get that and then reverse engineer it?**

Yeah, that's exactly how I do it. For me it works because it allows me to stay motivated. It always comes back to the pain level for me. Everybody's got a pain level. You get sick, you go to the doctor and they say, "What's your pain level at?" Say is it a one or a ten being the worst. When I had a kidney stone I was at a ten. When I worked for other people and followed their rules and took orders for people, my pain level was at a ten. When you have a high pain level, you'll do anything to be productive to get out of that pain level won't you.

For me personally, the pain level of having a boss or having somebody tell me how much money I can make and what I've got to work on and all those things is at a ten. That's why the productivity comes about when I just say wow, if I don't bust my butt, if I'm not productive, if I don't follow the things I need to do then I'm not going to be able to have this lifestyle anymore and that's what keeps me productive.

 Yeah, that makes total sense. I recently moved into the entrepreneurial realm after twenty years as a pastor of a church. Just recently the rubber's hit the road and it's come to a decision of we need more income, how can I do that. The thought of going to get a forty hour a week job where somebody else tells me what to do is just painful. It's really motivated me to get things rolling and it's been amazing what happens when you have that kind of motivation.

Exactly.

 I get what you're saying. The next question has to do with mindsets, since this book is about mind hacks. How do you think about work and self-discipline that it takes in order to work diligently?

How do I think?

 Yeah, how do you think about work? Is it a joy? Is it something that's a pleasure?

Yeah, because I love what I do now. I've designed my business around the lifestyle that I want. I can tell you the longer story is years and years ago I was sitting at my desk and I was on the phone with a client. I had younger kids at the time. I was talking to a client on the phone. All of a sudden my heart begin to pump really high and I started to get dizzy. I didn't know what was going on. I said to my client, "I have to go; something's wrong with me," and I hung up the phone. I sat there at my desk and I thought I was dying. My head was spinning, my heart was pumping out of my chest.

Long story short, I recovered from it later that afternoon, went to the doctor, did the full test and all that stuff. Sitting on the doctor's table and the doctor looked at me and said, "Jim, your problem is not here," pointing to my heart. "Your problem's here," pointing to my head. I had my first anxiety attack.

What I realized right after that was I was working way too hard on things I hated doing, for clients that I didn't like. Yes, I was making more money and yes, I was doing all those things, but it wasn't what I wanted. The mindset completely changed.

I got rid of the clients that I didn't want to work with. I made a complete switch to changing to a business model that I enjoyed doing and doing things that I liked helping people with and stop focusing on trying to copy other people's business models and do what other people have done to be successful. That's the mindset that has to happen if you want to get to that lifestyle point.

It doesn't happen for everybody and it usually takes a triggering event like an anxiety attack or something else. I guess I've never been addicted to any substance but from people who have, you hear them say that when you have your rock bottom moment, that triggering event that gets you to go to rehab or get some counseling or something like that, thing begin to change.. I'm not comparing the two at all. I'm just saying that everyone has a triggering event in their life that causes them to change their mindset, and that was mine. That's what changed me into being the lifestyle entrepreneur that I am today.

 Yeah, that totally makes sense. This one may seem a little more psycho-babble-ish but I believe that people have beliefs about themselves, whether they're positive or negative, that affect their ability to be productive. Have you been able to identify any things like that about yourself that you think either promote or limit your productivity?

I know that I'm a little bit lazy. I don't like to work constantly. Even if it's something I love doing I have a threshold of how much work I really want to do. That limits my ability to make a lot of money. I don't care about money, I don't. I care about my family. I care about making a living enough that I can do the things that I want to do.

The other thing that I believe that is something I need to change about myself is to get in shape. I'm overweight. I don't eat particularly well. I don't work out as much as I should. I do actually believe that if I was to change my body I would be able to be a more productive person because there are many people who have said that once you get into the mindset of being healthier, that helps with your clarity and focus and everything. I have flaws like everybody does and I realize those. You try to improve those.

 Sure. I can add another testimony to your bucket load. My wife and I lost fifty pounds each about three years ago. Man, it made a huge difference in my ability to focus and stay on track.

That's great.

Pre-plan meals and snacks

Andrea Beltrami

Feed the body with satisfying food and you'll nourish the mind at the same time.

It's no secret we need to eat the right food to give our bodies the fuel it needs to function at its highest state. But often cooking, especially healthy meals, takes more time than we have.

Or so we like to think.

The truth is that healthy doesn't have to be hard.

A great way to save time preparing meals without sacrificing nutrients or taste is to pre-make and package snacks and meals for the week.

For instance, I set aside an hour or so every Sunday night to prepare 3-4 different snacks and meals that I will eat throughout the week. This includes things like cutting up fruit for my morning smoothie, preparing and packaging my own "frozen dinners" (*i.e turkey meatballs and whole wheat pasta, chicken stir fry, black bean burritos*), even cooking a small chicken or turkey that I can use for sandwiches and salads.

Whenever hunger strikes while I'm hard at work during the week, I don't have to skip meals to save time, or worse, simply grab the ever-handy, though incredibly unhealthy, junk food.

Prepping your food beforehand will help you regain hours in your week, give your mind and body the fuel it needs to stay laser focused all day, and keep you from getting bogged down with meal choices or a lot of cook time while you're in your zone.

QUICK TIP:

When opportunity knocks, you need to

A.C.T.

A - Assess whether it will move you toward your business goals. Yes? Take the next step. No? Forget it.

C - Consider the costs in time, energy, creativity, resources, etc. Is this a "do it now" opportunity or a "someday, maybe" dream?

T - Take action. It will become someone else's opportunity if you don't get moving!

You need a system for everything

Carey Green

All you have to do to realize that life works better when it is governed according to systems is to look around you. Nature itself works according to systems.

Most of the stuff you learned about in 5th grade science class operates according to a system.

Systems are step by step, repeatable patterns that organize random things.

Systems bring order to chaos, then repeat that ordered pattern over and over, accomplishing amazing results.

You operate according to systems too.

Think about your morning routine for a minute. If you are like 99% of the people on the planet, you probably do the same things every morning, in the same order, in the same way.

I'll give you an example:

- The alarm goes off
- I get out of bed
- I answer the call of nature[9]
- I walk into the family room
- I get the fireplace going (*in the winter*)
- I start the hot water for tea
- I sit down with my Bible and journal

Later on, after I'm done with some very important personal time, I automatically click into another routine:

- I go into the bathroom
- I brush my teeth
- I fix my hair
- And on, and on

You get the point.

Let's drill into that morning routine a bit further and you'll see that the way you brush your teeth is systematic too.

_____

[9] My kids would say, "TMI, Dad!"

You start on the same side of your mouth, with your toothbrush held a certain way, etc. You've done it the same way so many times you do it without even thinking.

Why did you develop that particular tooth brushing routine?

It's because you discovered that it worked well for you. So you kept doing it.

THAT is called a habit.

And a **habit** is the beauty of a system.

Isn't that what you're really wanting; some habitual way to handle the tasks, demands, pressures, and responsibilities of life?

A habit that actually works in your favor?

I'm pretty certain that's why you opened this book in the first place. You want your life and business to work smoothly, according to a plan, so that you can produce something meaningful.

Am I right?

If you get the right systems in place, the ones that fit you... and if you can learn to use them habitually, you'll see the chaos that life can be become an organized pattern that produces amazing results.

But one size does NOT fit all.

There are many, many, many organizational and productivity systems out there. You won't have any trouble finding somebody to tell you that their way is the "best" way.

But I don't believe that. Not across the board, anyway.

What I believe is that you can find the best system for you but it may not be the best system for someone else.

The system that is right for you has to do with how God has wired you; how you think, process information, handle stress, and a thousand other things.

You'll probably even find a system that works for you "most of the time" but you'll have to make some tweaks to it so that it fits you better. That's what I've wound up doing.

I use most of the principles and guidelines of the Getting Things Done system. But even using a well thought-out system like GTD, I have had to adjust some things to fit me and my particular responsibilities. I've also had to adjust the philosophy of the system that I didn't quite agree with.

Getting basic

I find it helpful when ideas or concepts are broken down into their most basic components. I'm better able to get my brain around it then, better able to understand what it is and how it works. So that's what I'm going to do for you in this section.

For some of you deep, critical thinkers, my breakdown will seem overly simplistic, and it probably will be, for you.

But I'm willing to bet that my simple breakdown of what a system is, will help most people get it. So, here it comes:

A SYSTEM =

STEPS THAT LEAD TO AN END RESULT

Do you see it?

Step A leads to Step B, which results in C.

That's it. Nothing fancy, nothing difficult.

A system could have two or three steps like I've just described, or it could have hundreds of steps. The more steps a system has the more complex of a system it is. That makes sense, right?

If you can think of systems on this very basic level - step one, to step two, to step three, etc. - you'll be able to think through the more complex systems and break them down into their component steps more easily. That's important for goal setting and creating your own systems.

So, let's make up an example of a system you might see in an office environment.

ILLUSTRATION: Sue works at ABC Company as an Administrative Assistant. One of her responsibilities is to see that monthly updates are added to the company website on the 20th of every month. Her system for accomplishing that might look something like this:

- Remind department heads that updates are required. (*To do on the 10th*).
- Collect updates as they come in.
- File the updates until 15th.
- On 15th, organize updates into a logical sequence.
- Create a master sheet of updates.
- Email master update sheet to the webmaster.
- Follow up with webmaster on 17th to ensure that updates were received and will be posted on the 20th.
- If needed, help webmaster work through delays or difficulties.
- On 20th, report to boss that updates are done.

I could give you tons of examples of responsibilities in my own life that require a system.

- Podcast recording, editing, and publishing
- Writing a blog post
- Writing a novel or non-fiction book
- Publicizing upcoming books
- Planning time with my wife or kids
- Studying the scriptures
- Preparing a presentation for a speaking engagement
- Doing the editing and production work on a client's podcast
- Planning a marriage counseling intensive

Every single one of those is a thing that I deal with on a regular basis. And every one of them has a system behind it that enables me to get it done on time and with a consistent level of quality.

Every task needs a system

There are a handful of vital reasons that every task needs a system. Here are my top 7:

1. FOCUS

Systems enable you to stay on track, cut down on distractions, and get done what needs to get done.

2. RELIABILITY

Systems ensure that tasks are done routinely or according to deadlines.

3. CONSISTENCY

Systems ensure that nothing vital to the desired outcome is missed or overlooked.

4. QUALITY

Systems ensure that the task is done to the same degree of quality every time.

5. TRANSFERRABILITY

A good system is easily taught to a new person because it is a 1-2-3 process that anyone can learn. The only exception to this is when the task produced by the system requires an individual with certain technical skills.

6. EFFICIENCY

When a system is maximized it enables you to work more efficiently, accomplishing more work in less time with a higher degree of quality.

7. CONFIDENCE

Systems provide the peace of mind that comes from knowing that everything that needs to be done will be done.

There are probably many other benefits to setting up a system for every task but these are the biggies. Can you see how your life and business might be different if you can put some finely-tuned systems into place?

No more stress.

No more worry.

No more anxiety about quality, or production, or deadlines.

Your systems work for you, to enable you to accomplish the things you need to accomplish.

How to create a system

Systems are not very hard to create. It only requires time and some mental energy. Let's do a silly little example to get your mental juices flowing.[10]

EXAMPLE: Take out a sheet of paper right now. Go ahead, I'll wait.

Now, write this at the top of the page:

"System to make a peanut butter and jelly sandwich."

Now what do you think I'm going to have you do? That's right, I want you to write out the steps required to make a peanut butter and jelly sandwich, from the very beginning until its ready to be eaten.

I'm serious. There *is* a point to it. Ready? Go![11]

OK, did you get it done? Here's mine:

SYSTEM TO MAKE A PEANUT BUTTER & JELLY SANDWICH

- Walk to the pantry

---

[10] I know, "mental juices" sounds like the name of a mixed drink, but it's all I could come up with.

[11] If you rolled your eyes, skipped ahead without creating the PBJ system, or did something else instead, ask yourself this question: "Why?"

- Remove the loaf of bread & place it on the counter
- Walk to the refrigerator
- Take out the peanut butter. Take out the jelly. Place them on the counter
- Walk to the drawer & take out a butter knife and a spoon
- Open the loaf of bread and remove two slices of bread
- Open the jar of peanut butter
- Pick up the butter knife. Using the knife, remove some peanut butter from the jar
- Pick up one slice of bread
- Spread the peanut butter on one side of the piece of bread
- Repeat step 8 & step 10 until the bread is covered adequately
- Put the bread down
- Put down the knife
- Open the jar of jelly
- Pick up the second piece of bread
- Pick up the spoon and use it to remove some jelly from the jar
- Spread the jelly on the bread. Repeat if needed
- Put down the spoon
- Pick up both slices of bread & place them together, peanut butter & jelly sides facing inward
- Eat your sandwich!

OK, I hope you paid attention. There are some very important lessons to be learned about systems from this very simple example.

First - *systems have to be very detailed*

I'm almost certain that there were steps on my list that you didn't include on yours, simple things like "pick up the knife." You didn't put them on your list because they seemed like "givens" to you. Naturally, you are going to pick up the knife before you spread the peanut butter on the bread, right?

But you can't think that way when you create a system.

If you do, you'll lose some of the benefits I mentioned a few pages ago, things like the consistency of your outcome, the quality of your end result, and the transferability of your process. Let's break those down.

CONSISTENCY - If your system doesn't contain every single step then the folks who actually put the system to work will begin to vary the process. It won't happen on purpose but it will happen, and the lack of clarity will produce varied results.

QUALITY - Naturally, if the process used to get to the end result varies, the quality of the end result will vary as well.

TRANSFERABILITY - If you aren't clear on what it takes to do the process the way you want it done, you won't be able to transfer the process to a new person effectively.

And we're talking about a peanut butter and jelly sandwich.

Think what a difference variations in your system could make when you're making widgets, or semiconductors, or websites.

Second - *systems can and should be tweaked*

All my talk about not varying the process may have led you to believe that a system checklist is a "carved in stone" kind of thing that can never be changed.

That's not true at all.

In fact, systems should be continually fine-tuned so that you can optimize them for efficiency and quality.

If you look back at my PB&J checklist, you'll see where I did exactly that toward the end of the list. I combined some steps in the later part of the exercise that I did not combine in the earlier part of the exercise.

Take the next to the last step, for example. I could have written it out as three different steps but realized that I could combine things and have less steps in the process. So I did.

Take some time to look over my list. Can you find places where the system could be changed to make it even more efficient or easier to understand?

That's called "tweaking" the system (*my technical term, there*)[12]. It's being in control of the system so that you are able to constantly refine and maximize it. *The better your systems become the more effective they will be.*

For those of you who work in an organization that is more than a one-man/woman show, consider this:

Whenever you build a system, you should also create a built-in way for those who are using it to suggest tweaks in order to make it better.

---

[12] I have lots of technical terms like this: cranking, busting, jazzed, and podunked among them.

Not only will you be improving your systems, you'll also be giving the folks who use them ownership in the process. That will make for happier, more content system-workers.

Third - *systems have to be followed*

Because you've made a peanut butter and jelly sandwich before, you could break away from your system list and still get the sandwich made with no trouble. That's fine.

But systems that bring order out of chaos can't be treated that way. *They have to be followed.*

> **Stepping away from a good system is like taking a back alley to your destination when you have no idea where the alley leads.**

Good systems are road maps to your desired outcome. They are created to ensure that you get there. If you want to get to the place you are going, stick to the system.[13]

---

[13] I have been known to ignore the GPS on my phone at times, but I do so because I haven't had enough experience with GPS to

Fourth - *systems should be written down*

How are you going to transfer a system to a new person if it's not written down?

How are you going to remind yourself of the vital steps included in a project or task if it's not written down?

How are you going to do quality checks to make sure you didn't skip an important step if you didn't write it down?

You must, must, must write down your systems.

That's one reason I call it a "systems check list." It communicates that I must have a list in front of me to guide me to the end result.

Really? Every task needs a system?

You may think that some things don't require a system; things like, "How to answer the

---

fully trust it yet. You may be that way with your systems at first. Just keep tweaking them. You'll learn to trust them in time.

phone," or "How to put paper in the copier," or "How to change the toilet paper."[14]

On some levels, you're probably right. There is a point where a system for everything becomes borderline obsessive-compulsive.

I said you need a system for "every task" at first because I wanted you to see the important benefits that systems can bring to every task. Now that you see that (*you do see it, don't you?*), I'm going to back off a bit. Here's what I'll say instead:

Make sure that every task or responsibility that directly impacts the quality of your desired outcomes has its own system.

Do I sound a little less obsessive now?

You know your business, life, and responsibilities better than I do so you have to decide on your outcomes and how you're going to get to them (*your systems*).

But I can tell you this; if you allow things to be done willy-nilly-however-any-employee-wants,

---

[14] I know, most of you women think ALL of us men need the toilet paper system. Hey, you know what? If you send me one, I just might consider it... as long as I have permission to tweak it.

then you're going lose every one of the benefits that a system brings.

Flexibility is vital

The previous few sections may have given you the idea that systems are fairly rigid. They can be but don't have to be. In fact, if a system is too rigid it will not be able to handle reality as it is.

Think about it:

Situations and circumstances change all the time.

Employees and workers come and go.

Nothing stays the same.

Because of that fact your systems can't either.

Systems have to be adaptive to handle the movements and surges of life and business. It's your job to make sure they adapt when needed.

What YOU have to bring to the system.

I realize that I've made systems sound kind of like "magical" things that enable you to do tons more than you thought possible. I want you to know that I'm not over-blowing the power of good systems.

It's really true.

But there is one thing that no system can provide for you. This one thing is something *you* have to bring to the table, something *you* have to learn and use day after day after day as you are working within the systems you create.

What is it?

Self-discipline

No system will work if

YOU won't work it.

You have to sit down, get out your systems checklist, and do the steps required to fulfill that responsibility, every single day.

If you don't, you'll lose the benefits systems bring and you'll fall back into that rut of non-productivity.

You don't want to go there.

So teach yourself the hard skill of self-discipline here, at the front end.

Go public with your projects

Rick Eliason

I am an ideas guy.

My mind never shuts off, my phone is full of thoughts and notes to myself. I have scraps of paper with scribblings in every corner of my flat and dry-wipe boards with ideas that have been there so long the boards are permanently stained.

What I have found hard in my life is not starting projects. (*Eat That Frog* by Brian Tracy *sorted that*) My problem has been finishing them.

Particularly long ones where the glitter of the idea has faded and it feels like a long slog to the finish line.I have found one method that has really helped and that is this:

Tell as many people you care about as possible about your project.

Or find a public portal and blast it out if necessary. Scream it from the rooftops. Detail exactly what people can expect from the final product and set goals and deadlines. By doing so it is much harder to ignore or fail. You are no longer just letting yourself down - you are letting others down and that is harder to confront.

Take my #googleplus50 project for example.

If I was at home writing one big offline document I would never have got past #5.

But I had:
- created a frequented landing page that was linked to from the rest of my site
- made a Google+ cover image that advertised the series
- gathered an expectant following
- told loads of people about it
- got colleagues interested
- told my clients etc.

Because I did all those things there was no backing out. Although each post took around an hour to research and write for 50 days straight (*almost*) I had a vested interest and support from many other people. I didn't want to fail them.

The result was 5000+ new followers, features, and mentions all over the web, and lots of other good opportunities.

I know I would never have completed the series had I kept it to myself. For anyone that struggles with keeping on track and self-motivation I implore you to do this!

QUICK TIP:

Things worth doing take time...

but if they take too much time your intensity might begin to wane to unproductive levels.

This little jewel comes from

Cal Newport

Rethinking your to-do list

Julie Coraccio

One of the biggest changes I made to my business was tackling my to-do list.

Before I was really regimented and had to do A, B, and C, regardless of how I felt. I now use a big notebook where I write down all of the items I must do.

Each morning I ask myself "What do I need to do today?" Then I listen. Each day I can be in the flow I am happier because I am in the present moment listening to myself at the deepest levels.

I need to schedule clients, interviews and events, and I can't do this 24/7. What has happened though, is that I am able to do this more and more, and what needs to be scheduled flows together a lot more easily.

The key is staying fluid. When you have the flexibility to ask what needs to be done, you honor that. If you practice this regularly, you will find you are getting more work done in less time and are much less stressed about it.

Exercise:
- One day this week sit quietly and ask yourself what you feel like doing today.
- If it's on your to-do list, great, if not, that is okay, too.
- Honor what your gut is telling you to do and see if that enables you to be more productive.

Systems are not the goal. Goals are.

Carey Green

So far, I've talked a lot about the importance of systems, for good reason; systems are what keep you organized and on track.

But systems are not an end in themselves. Systems serve the outcomes you want to see happen, the things you're heading toward.[15]

There's lots of debate about what to call these far-off things: visions, dreams, ambitions, purpose? I just call them goals.

Goals are what matter.

Goals are the final outcome you're heading toward. If you don't have goals, you're doing a lot of work without a clearly defined reason for why you're doing it.

Goals are:

---

[15] It's like communication in marriage. It's a good, vital thing - but it's not the goal. Marital intimacy is the goal. Communication just helps us get there.

- The end of the race
- The light at the end of the tunnel
- The happy end to a long, agonizing struggle
- The meaningful purpose you want to se come from your life and your efforts.
- The reward for long, hard, diligent effort

The power of a good goal

When I was a kid, I played a lot of baseball. It was normal for me and my friends to head to the ball park on a Saturday morning and spend the whole day there.

There was a time in my life, which comes for most kids who play baseball, when I thought I wanted to be a professional baseball player when I grew up. It was a nice childhood dream, but nothing more than a dream.

I can see now that it wasn't something I really, really wanted. I wasn't willing to put in the necessary hard work to achieve it. It was "wishful thinking," something that would be nice if it happened, but OK if it didn't.

But later on, when I was in the 8th grade, I had a very different experience, and it didn't have to do with baseball.

I had been in the percussion section of the school band since sixth grade. You know, snare drum, bass drum, cymbals, triangle... all the noisemakers in the back that keep the rest of the band on track (*or at least that's what we were supposed to do*).

It was OK, but nothing like what I was about to experience.

I went to my first high school basketball game because my older brother was playing trombone in the Stage Band at halftime. The stage band was like a rock-pop band with brass instruments, electric guitars, and drums. You know, "Tonight Show" kind of stuff (*google it*).

The Stage Band played cover tunes from bands like Chicago, Toto, Steely Dan, and others... and it was very cool.[16]

Watching and listening to the stage band something happened to me. Or maybe I should say "someone" happened to me.

_____

[16] Yes it was!

It was the drummer.

The guy's name was Mike Schneider and he was very, very good. The magic he produced with two wooden sticks and a drum set grabbed me like nothing else.

I began attending the basketball games every week and stood on the balcony above Mike. I can still see him below me, smoothly playing his fills and easing right back into a perfect beat to keep the band driving forward. The crowd went crazy when he played his weekly drum solo.

One day my brother mentioned that Mike would be graduating at the end of the year. That meant he wouldn't be playing for the stage band the next year and there was nobody else in the high school band who played the drum set.

ZING!

That's when the goal became clear for me. I wanted to be the next drummer for the stage band.

I didn't only dream about being the drummer in the stage band the next year, I set a goal. And I created a system to take me to my goal.

Here's the basics of what I did:

- I spoke to the high school band director to get permission to audition for the position (*Freshman weren't usually allowed to be in the Stage Band*). He said, "OK, you can at least try out."
- I talked my mother into buying me a beat-up, mismatched drum set from the local pawn shop.
- I also struck a deal with my mom: If I won the audition she would buy me a still-used-but-newer drum set. I'm not sure what she was thinking, but she agreed.
- I took my cheapo Realistic cassette tape recorder to the basketball games and recorded every song the Stage Band played and I watched Mike carefully as I listened.
- I sat up my junker drum set in the garage, put on my cheesy little one-ear

earplug speaker and practiced all summer long, teaching myself how to play the drum set.

- At the audition I was selected to be the lead drummer for the Stage Band.

Goal reached.[17]

How do you tell the difference between a dream and a goal?

You know the difference by answering this question: "Is this something I'm willing to work for until I achieve it, no matter what it takes?"

If you answer, "No," then it's only wishful thinking. If you answer "Yes," then it's a genuine goal.

Have you ever set a goal and reached it?

- How did it feel?
- How did you enjoy the fruit of your labor differently than if you'd been given what you worked for?

What goals are you shooting for now?

---

[17] And I've played the drums in church and other settings ever since.

- Do you have a system in place to reach it?

Batch tasks for efficiency

Andrea Beltrami

It's not your ability to multi-task that increases productivity but the ability to create plans and structure. Planning is the key to success in most areas of life and it's no different when we're talking about our level of productivity and our ability to complete a great number of things in a day, week, month or year.

One way to leverage planning and cut down on the time a task takes is to group the same tasks together.

For instance, I create blog posts 2-3 months at a time. For example, I outline all the topics, I research all the SEO keywords, I write all of the copy, I create all of the visual content and collate it into a cohesive package.

Instead of going through that process each week I batch tasks together and get months of work done in a week or two and then I have the next 2-3 months free to promote that content, connect and engage with others, and tackle the next project on my to do list.

Productivity is all about systems and efficiency!

Doing each task in batch mode allows you to effortlessly stay in a zone (*i.e you need to be in a different mind-space to write than you do when designing visual content*) and make efficient use of your limited time rather than flitting between unstructured tasks.

Batching your work and tasks will also help you create systems and processes for your frequent and repetitive tasks. Which in turn, will greatly increase your level of productivity and decrease the hours it takes to accomplish those tasks.

Not to mention, it's quite a bit easier to outsource those tasks later on, to say an assistant, as there's now a proven framework for them to follow.

QUICK TIP:

One of the milestones every entrepreneur passes is when she stops thinking of people she hires as expensive ("I could do that job for free") and starts thinking of them as cheap ("This frees me up to do something more profitable.")

A gold nugget from

SETH GODIN

Misplaced action in your business

Stephanie Calahan

Sometimes taking action is not the right choice.

I have been thinking about that statement for a while now.

It seems funny for me to say it because I'm continually telling people they need to get out of perfectionism and procrastination and into action. Just do something!

However, I'm reminded that not all action is good action. It is worth looking into here though, because it is an important point to understand.

#1 I believe taking action is better than not taking action. If you take action you can evaluate and regroup when necessary.

#2 When you take action, consider *why* you are taking action and make sure you are good habits for your business.

You see, it is not *just* about taking *any* action. One of my quotes that gets shared frequently is "You can be busy all day and still have gotten nothing done."

Do you feel that? Can you relate? So often, we are just busy being busy. That does not necessarily equal progress.

Being productive means that you are taking action on things that are LEADING you to something.

Here is a story to illustrate:

Say you own a business and you have a salesperson that continues to come by to try to sell you something you are not interested in. The sales person (*let's call him Bill*) is not very good at sales, so his supervisor sends him to a motivational seminar to increase his drive.

Bill comes back from his motivational seminar raring to go! He has reaffirmed his goals and is ready to hit the streets hard! He is *motivated* but this motivation is external to him.

That sounds good right? Except that we've forgotten one thing, he does not know *how* to sell.

So, Bill continues to work his sales route, but now he's driven to take more action than before. Unfortunately, since he does not know how to sell, all you experience is a sales person that will not leave you alone and is bugging you more than ever.

Bill, is working harder than ever and is experiencing less results!

Hmmm... in this instance action did not work.

This is where taking time to step back and get to the root of your issue (*in this case Bill not knowing how to sell*) is critical. Bill had not needed motivational training, he needed sales training. The action was misplaced.

I work with entrepreneurs, coaches, consultants, trainers, healers, speakers and other powerful messengers who are really amazing at what they do and have achieved great success in their business - but have done so at the expense of their personal freedom or well-being and happiness, which makes them feel over-worked and out of balance; or limited in terms of growth as their business lacks scalability.

They get into what I have talked about before. That hamster wheel where they are going and going but not getting the traction they want. Often times that is due to misplaced action.

If you find that you are working but you're not getting where you want to go, or your message is not getting out in the way that you would like, maybe you have misplaced action too.

Step back and evaluate, then begin moving forward again.

If you would like help figuring that out, reach out to a coach that can help you see what you may not be able to see on your own.

Onward!

Productivity starts before I punch the clock.

Susan Finch

As entrepreneurs and CEOs, we don't have a set schedule. But I personally find that I need to block-out time for specific tasks or I can get swallowed up by spontaneity, multi-tasking and randomness. Those things keep me from accomplishing what needs to be done.

I find this especially important because I work from home in what used to be the dining area. The possible distractions are many. But, as this is world headquarters for Susan Finch Solutions and my family, I have trained my team (*my two children*), since the time they were very small, that work time is quiet time, and I can't always drop everything to attend to their whims.

To make sure I accommodate them they have also been coached that I *can* schedule around my tasks to be available for them with advanced notice. Whether at home or in the office, time blocks and boundaries help with creating a productive - and satisfying - day.

Blocking out time to prepare for my day is one of my keys to productivity.

From 6-7 am Monday through Friday, I take time to start my day by preparing our home for my family, with a focus on the kitchen in particular. When they wake up and get ready for a successful day at school, I want them to know that I have considered them first. They deserve that positive mindset.

These are small items, but they definitely have an effect, whether my family realizes it or not. I see the difference in how our mornings go when I do these simple tasks in the morning:

- Table cleaned and welcoming for them.
- Cats and dog fed so they don't pester anyone.
- Kitchen floor and counter cleared of clutter.
- Dishwasher emptied - this is *totally* so that I can see a bit of completion at the start of my day - physical evidence of success. Even though it is very small, matters to *me*.
- Vitamins are out and available.

Taking care of those family tasks first leaves me time to get my computer booted up and scanned, and I'm able to check in with my volunteer tasks.

I am proud to run a 501c3 organization called Binky Patrol Comforting Covers for Kids. We make blankets and give them away to children and teens across the country. We have over 120 chapters currently.

That means that the chapters around the country need my support and encouragement. There are also taxes, reports and other "non-blanket-making" activities that require my attention each week. This hour is for *that* time.

My husband and I teach art as volunteers at my children's school, so I also use that hour for planning art projects. If I'm mentoring someone, or helping a friend with a video, script, proposal, etc. outside of work, this is when I do that as well. I make an effort to keep this hour flexible and take advantage of the time to also manage my focused marketing tasks such as blog posts, newsletters, promo videos, editing and graphics.

7am: On duty at home again:

With the first hour behind me, I am ready to greet my family with a warm, sincere "good morning," a hug, smile and my full attention I am theirs without distraction. That means I don't pay attention to my cell phone or email, until they leave for the bus at 8:00.
That's when the billable work begins.

At that time, I wrap up the volunteer and passion projects and move into client mode. I'm ready to continue to be of service to my clients, who have put their trust in me.

In 1988 I worked at an advertising agency in Orange County called Roberts, Mealer, Emerson. Jack Mealer was at the helm and the lifeblood of the agency. His level of humility and integrity took root in my consciousness. One year, he had mugs printed for our break room and to send to every client. They read, "Our customers do not need us, we need our customers. Be of service."

As I approach each client, I am constantly reminded of the simple message on that coffee mug. I am also reminded of the priest who officiated my wedding, Father Eamon O'Gorman. He asked us one question that would forever set the tone of that day *and* our marriage:

> **"Are you to be the honored guests or the gracious hosts?"**

Think about that question for a few moments.

Are we to be SERVED or be of SERVICE?

This is my mind hack, my recipe for success.

It comes into play each day online through my connections, my feedback, my comments, my emails, and my mindset with clients.

It plays into my in-person connections and how I listen and am *present* for others.

It most sincerely affects my family as we set the tone with our children, to reinforce how valuable they are to us and how much they matter and resonate with us.

I have carried that with me since. With a mindset of love and service to each other, you cannot help but be successful.

I tell it to myself and others regularly to check their motives.

Why are you doing something? Why are you *saying* or *writing* something? Only you can answer your motives. Sometimes it takes practice to be that honest with yourself.

As you sit down and reflect, remember Father O'Gorman's question: "Are you an honored guest, or a gracious host?"

Discover your own rhythms

Donnie Byrant

It's true: the early bird does catch the worm.

It's also true that eagles catch fish in the afternoon and owls catch field mice at night.

In my first couple years an entrepreneur, I felt the pressure to be an early riser. I was told that 'early to rise' was the way to squeeze the most productive time into each day. Guilt would eat me up whenever I didn't get out of bed before 6am.

After a couple years of beating myself up for not fitting into what I thought was the proper entrepreneurial mold, *I realized that energy management is just as important as time management.*

One of the beautiful things about being an entrepreneur is that you get to make your own rules and set your own agenda. That includes when, where and how you do your work.

Here's the point: everyone is unique.

In fact, there's evidence that early risers and night owls have different brain structures. Check out this article by Michael J. Breus, PhD.

Discover your own "rhythms" and schedule your most important/profitable tasks for those times when you are naturally most energetic, alert and powerful. You'll find yourself becoming much more productive and creative.

For me, I feel like I can conquer the world between 8pm and 1am most days. If it makes sense to spend our time on our strengths instead of our weaknesses, doesn't it also make sense to align our priority activities with the times our minds and bodies are feeling the strongest?

recommended PRODUCTIVITY VIDEOS

- How to Get Productive on a Project in 24 Hours (1:01:02)

- Get Your Projects Completed (a talk by Scott Belsky) (10:45)

- Hour-Tracking for Priority Optimization (7:55)

- Engaged Productivity and the Art of Discardia (8:27)

- The Art of Stress-Free Productivity (David Allen) (22:16)

- Double Your Productivity (8:44)

- 7 Brain Hacks to Improve Your Productivity (2:18)

- How Millionaires Schedule Their Day (with Brendon Burchard) (30:57)

- 7 Secrets to Super-charge Your Productivity (14:00)

- <u>Becoming the Ultimate Productivity Ninja</u> (1:55)

recommended PRODUCTIVITY PODCASTS

- [My Top 10 Productivity Hacks](#) (Michael Hyatt)

- [Jon Acuff on Routines, Work Spaces, and Hustle](#)

- [Ray Edwards on Focus, Productivity, and Deadlines](#)

- [4 Essential Habits for Getting Things Done](#)

- [Not-to-do lists, Drugs, and other Productivity Tricks](#) (Tim Ferris)

- [The Quick and Dirty Tips: Get Er Done Guy](#) (I couldn't pick one episode).

- [The Best GTD Strategies for Ultimate Productivity](#) (Jeff Sanders)

- [The iProcrastinate Podcast](#) (again, how can you pick just one?)

Here's the section where we talk about

CREATIVITY

Learn to see what others miss

Carey Green

Seeing what others miss is natural for some people.

Take Seth Godin for example. He's very adept at noticing things that others either overlook or are unwilling to talk about. Jesus was the same way (*only better at it*).

In fact, almost every visionary, inventor, major scientist, or inspiring leader has been able to see things that others don't. It doesn't matter if they are a positive example (*Nelson Mandela*) or a negative one (*Adolph Hitler*). They see opportunities, needs, causes, weaknesses, wrongs, situations, etc. through eyes that seek a way to capitalize on them - for good or bad.

But I believe that kind of creativity is a skill that can be learned too.

Everybody can and should train themselves to notice what is typically unnoticed. Each of us has a unique mix of gifts, skills, and abilities that we are supposed to use to make a positive difference in the world. It's our calling, our destiny. But we've got to put on a different pair of glasses than we were handed at birth if we're going to pull it off.

Becoming adept at seeing the unseen is nothing more than developing keen skills of observation, like the fictional Sherlock Holmes. It's unique observations that can make a huge difference in how you view the world and how you operate in it.

But it's also about knowing how to interpret the things you see.

- What do the things you notice say, show, or mean for the people around them?

- What impact do they have on the present and the future?

- What would changes to them provide or prohibit?

- How can they be improved to maximize their benefits?

When you learn to do this consistently you'll begin to see a handful of powerful results.

1. You'll begin to find your place in the world (*maybe*).

2. You'll find problems to fix or solve.

3. You'll find beautiful, wonderful things about life you didn't know were there.

4. You'll begin to differentiate yourself from your competition in important ways.

5. You'll learn to serve customers, clients, friends, and family better.

How to learn to see

I've experimented with this concept many times in my life and have picked up a few tips that I'd like to pass on.

TAKE TIME TO LOOK

Noticing things takes time, at least at first. Consider your daily commute or a drive you make quite often. Can you tell me the color of the 3rd building you see? What about the type of font used on the sign at the local grocery store?

These things may sound insignificant, and probably are, but they illustrate how little we truly stop to look around us.

One reason you don't notice things on that drive is because you're moving too fast. If you were to walk the same route instead of driving, you'd have time to see things you normally miss.

That's my problem. I'm typically in such a mad dash to get something done that I pass by relevant, important things in the process.

Over the years I have tried to slow down, at least in my mind. I try to stop for a few seconds (*I can afford a few seconds*) to assess what it is that I'm seeing.

I try to notice colors, sounds, smells, shapes, textures, attitudes, habits, cultural norms, conversations... It's mind blowing when you begin to realize all the amazing things that you pass by every day.

TAKE TIME TO THINK

Once you've noticed something, start to analyze it. Ask yourself these types of questions:

- Does this work?
- Is it well-built?
- Did the designer think it through well?
- What is wrong with it?
- How could it be better?
- Is there an injustice happening here?
- Is there a need that could be/should be met here?
- Is it enjoyable? What could make it more so?
- Is there a lie or type of misinformation needing to be corrected?
- Is there a beauty that needs to be made much of?

You get the point.

Stop accepting what is as what must be.

Try to imagine what might be.

How could your particular insights into the thing or situation make it better?

What keeps you from noticing things that others miss?

Martin Shervington answers my questions about creativity

 Talk to me for a bit about creativity. How do you get into your creative spot where you're the most creative? What sorts of things do you need to do practically to get yourself there?

I need to play; and its playing with ideas.

What I've done for the last two and half years is, sometimes I'll be working on something and I'd get into it, and its play. I ask, "What can I do that's going to be fun? Not just for me to be doing but for other people in particular? How do I engage people around something?"

A lot of the campaigns that I do on Google Plus, it's like, "How do I make this an enjoyable experience; an enjoyable learning experience because obviously that's what we'll do?" Also, I do a lot of research. That's a lot of what the experimentation is about; so it is fun because you've got this endpoint over here where you could have one time 250,000 people visiting your website by using certain methodology. That's it.

How do I get into it? It's geek-ing out. For me, I go down rabbit holes. It's a painful pleasure because it's incredibly intense from a detail point of view. I think like a lot of people, I always look at the big picture. I'm a big picture person and it's like that's just because you're lazy about flicking into the detail. You've got to flick into the detail. Somebody's got to do the detail and if you haven't got other people that can do it, you've got to do it and that's what I've been doing.

It's "everything just needs to be done right," and you become, to some extent a perfectionist but you choose your perfectionism. However, not trying to make other people prefect is one of the things. You actually have to relax into allowing people to be as they are.

That's another thing; working with other people makes me more creative, so when there are multiple things and I can bounce around and ask, "What do you think about this?" That's another good way.

 **Do you have a process for how you evaluate what comes out of a creative time?**

Yeah. For me there's pretty much straightforward metrics, where if something goes into Google search, if the campaign has been about getting a search result how many website visitors have there been? How many website visitors are staying over time not just for social but search over a long time? How many views on a particular video on YouTube? How much social engagement directly within a platform?

Those are all the quantitative metrics from the qualitative side. Do people enjoy that thing that's being created? If they're part of the process, do they feel part of it? One of the biggest things that I found, is using this platform, using Google Plus, is that I have to be asking, "How can we make this a more creative experience?"

How do you set up the community differently? What's the emotional response by changing the categories? What about changing the image? Everything affects it.

 **It probably makes things much more engaging too, the connection within the community.**

Yeah, just from Trail Blazers community, this is another site which was the first paid community which we've done. After six weeks they trended number one on Google in the world by putting all the posts out that I gave them as an assignment to do.

Incredible creativity, hundreds of re-shares, they're all over the moon but they trended number one. I didn't go after that as an outcome but the evidence was of their creativity which I showed them how to do things. That's nice. That's really reassuring.

Step away from the computer.

<u>Phyllis Khare</u>

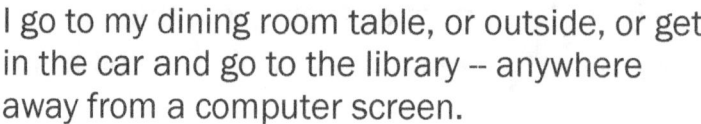

If I need to get into a creative mental space the first thing I do is step away from the computer.

I go to my dining room table, or outside, or get in the car and go to the library -- anywhere away from a computer screen.

Then I go all old-school with a large piece of paper and some markers. Yep. I find the best way to really dig deep into the next creative thing I'm developing is to pull out the artist in me.

I draw flow charts and boxes and arrows and then all the creative ideas start to flow. By the time I'm done I'll have a complete plan for my next product or book or whatever else I'm being asked to create.

Works every time. Once I have this lovely piece of artwork I transfer all of it onto my calendar to make sure it all gets done!

QUICK TIP:

"You can't use up creativity.
The more you use, the more you have."

Pearls of wisdom from

MAYA ANGELOU

Set your mind on the context

Dan Crask

One of my primary roles at Brand Shepherd is Creative Director, so I make my living from constantly being creative in the work we produce, as well as how we create it - the processes that go into running all of the working parts.

Hanging on a wall near my desk is a quote from one of my heroes in creativity, Walter Gropius, one of the founders of the German Bauhaus School of Design in the early 1900s. He said,

> **"Art is self-expression;**
>
> **Design is problem-solving."**

These words are the foundation of how I approach creativity.

The best mind hack I can offer for creativity is to *get your thinking right and apply it to the context you're in - not the context you wish you were in.*

Leading my fellow professional creatives in projects has taught me that getting over the battle of putting ourselves aside and engaging on behalf of our clients is the biggest challenge. But once we are in the mindset of our clients we get to help make their ideas come to life.

This is a lot tougher than it sounds.

In his prolific book on leading creatives, "The Heart of the Artist," Rory Noland writes that it is important to understand and accept that truly creative people are hardwired to be hypersensitive. If we were not hypersensitive, we could not create what we create.

Here is where I must point out something that will be uncomfortable and comfortable at the same time: Creativity is not an innate human characteristic that anyone can excel at. Some people really struggle to be creative. And I am here to say: It's ok. If just anyone could be truly creative, we would not have exceptional creatives in any profession and/or trade.

This brings us full-circle to mindset:

Knowing the context you are in, and not the one you wish you were in. If you wish you were

a truly creative person, but are not, embrace
what you are good at.

4 ways to sharpen your creative edge

Katrina Pfannkuch

It requires attention to keep a creative edge sharp. The little mindful things you do to stretch your imagination, open your heart, and shift how you see yourself connecting in the world are the real "sharpening tools" and lead you to your creative edge - if you are willing to go there.

However, when you are stuck in a rut, it isn't always easy to change just for the sake of changing.

Here are some simple ways to help crack open your defenses and break long-worn habits so that you can challenge yourself in a meaningful way to expand your creative edge.

1. Challenge yourself with something new rather than expanding the reach of a current goal.

What do you consider a challenge? A mental puzzle you need to figure out? A physical exertion of strength and endurance? Repairing a strained emotional connection?

When you know the type of challenge you like best, the type that plays to your strengths, be adventurous and pick something else to practice.

A creative sense of self is found in how you play with all aspects of your mind, body and spirit, so dabble in the less-polished skills to strengthen them. If one skill is over-developed, it's harder to feel grounded or capable in a situation that requires skills you never practice.

For example, if you always take on mental challenges, those creative edges are razor sharp. But it leaves other aspects of your creative center (*body and spirit*) dull and soft.

2. Be willing to be vulnerable.

Vulnerability starts with your willingness to look at what feels scary or impossible. Standing in a space where you are forced to share the truth about yourself, even with yourself, is one of the fastest ways to sharpen your creative edge. It puts the cards on the table in clear view and helps you take ownership of your dark spots - which can be very powerful creativity suckers!

Start by writing in a journal or creating artwork that expresses personal insecurities, or share something in a personal or group setting. Even quiet time alone with no distractions is an easy way to begin this practice.

In the big picture, vulnerability is a cornerstone of creative expression. What you say, do, or express, and how you do it are completely unique to you. There's no special formula to follow or "right way" to be vulnerable or creative. It's a risk you take to walk through one and get to the beauty and gifts of the other.

3. Acknowledge and honor your inner voice above all others.

Your inner voice shares insights and warnings. No matter where the advice leads you, it's yours, so own it! The more you get caught up in asking opinions, doing more research, or second guessing what you feel and hear in your heart, you are diluting the guidance you receive.

To sharpen your creative edge, practice listening to your inner voice. Will it always lead you to your ideal expected outcome? Not necessarily, but it will give you an opportunity to reach a new edge in self-trust through practice.

4. Believe in what you create - during the process and after it's complete.

A strong creative sense of self starts with believing in what you make. Before you measure your creative expression against the money it earns, how it's received by others, or by the amount of attention it gets, be proud of your effort and creative practice.

> **Everyone learns by doing. No exception.**

When you have a natural skill for something it still takes a willingness to believe in what you are creating during the process and after, even if it doesn't meet expectations. That's because it all starts with believing in your own expressions.

As you believe and trust more in your own unique creative process you are slowly and easily building a solid foundation to support you as you grow and sharpen your creative edge.

Find your creativity switch

Stephanie Calahan

For years, when I saw the word "creativity" I would think that it applied to other people, but not me. I looked at creativity in a very limited form. You see, my brothers got all of the creative genes in our family (*or so I thought*). They could create beautiful drawings and paintings, while the best I could do was stick figures.

That is the way it was, until I took a different look at creativity. Creativity is much broader than that! Creativity can be artistic, musical, out-of-the-box thinking, and a lot more.

Once I tuned-in to a different way of thinking about creativity, I was able to find my creativity switch.

My creative outlet is music. According to my parents, I have been singing almost since birth and I have played a number of instruments as well. For some crazy reason, I had looked at that part of me as something separate.

Today, I have made music an integral part of every day. I have experimented with a variety of genres of music and have found that different types influence my output in my work.

I have different playlists for when I write, work with graphics, prepare for client appointments, prepare to speak on stage, create new products and more! I have music to energize me and music to put me into a calm, meditative state.

The really fantastic thing about using this tool of music is that I can instantly jump myself into the mode of thinking I want, simply by playing tunes on my phone or computer. It goes wherever I go!

Over time I have helped my clients experiment with music too. I'd love to tell you that there is a one-size-fits-all solution: e.g. listen to X type of music and you'll be an amazing writer. Alas, that is not the case.

Different rhythms and combinations of notes will create different emotions for each listener. What is energizing to my creative flow may be irritating to you.

The best place to start is to think of a time where you were in flow with your creative genius. Try to tune into the feelings that you had when that was happening. Then, think of music that inspires the same kind of feelings when you listen to it. More than likely, that will be your creativity switch.

QUICK TIP:

"Make visible what, without you, may never have been seen."

Inspiration from

ROBERT BRESSON

Swipe files & inspiration files

Andrea Beltrami

I find the smallest things can jar loose the most amazing creativity, but it certainly doesn't happen on demand.

That's why I keep swipe files of inspiring things and save them for those times I get creatively blocked. In fact, some of my most profound content has been inspired from a simple quote or photograph.

Pinterest and Evernote are great tools for creating your swipe files and inspiration boards. Anytime you see something that inspires you, makes you laugh, or just moves you in some way, either pin it to one of your Pinterest boards or add it to an Evernote file.

Create boards and files and organize them by the type of content. For instance, you can create titles like these: email subjects lines, opt-in offers, blog post topics, logos, color palettes, and visual content you love.

Anytime you get stuck and need a creative jolt of inspiration it's just a couple clicks away.

It's important to set yourself up for success by planning for the struggles that are inevitable. We all get creativity blocks so plan for them. Use swipe files to create inspiration you can tap into whenever the need arises.

I bet you find your creative groove isn't as far away as you thought.

How to be exceptional in your niche

Carey Green

If you don't know about a guy by the name of Cal Newport, you need to.[18]

Cal is currently (*2014*) Assistant Professor of Computer Science at Georgetown University and blogs often on what he refers to as "deep work."

In this great post he highlights that there are two kinds of work - "knowlege work" and "deep work." How does he define them? Here's my paraphrase...

Knowledge work (*KW*) is primarily task-based work. It's the administrative stuff that every one of us has to do from time to time. It's the mundane stuff we all wish we could offload to a VA or employee.

Some things I have observed about knowledge work are:

---

[18] I should say "know of," since I don't personally know him myself.

- KW can be done in short bursts.
- KW can be interrupted without serious consequence.
- KW is typically completed without much creative effort.
- KW is accomplished relatively easily.
- KW doesn't require much endurance because its life-cycle from start to completion is fairly short.

> **Cal suggests that knowledge work is what takes up the majority of our time, because it's easy and makes us FEEL productive.**

As I've examined my own work habits I've found that to be true. Something in me gravitates toward getting a lot of minor things done rather than investing large amounts of time and creative energy in a larger project.

But knowledge work is not what will make me exceptional in my niche(s). Knowledge work will not bring out the best in me over the long haul.

Deep work (*DW*) is what does that. Cal defines deep work as "cognitively demanding activities that leverage our training to generate rare and valuable results, and that push our abilities to continually improve.[19]"

Deep work is hard because it requires concentration, diligence, endurance, and an eye for excellence. It goes against the grain of our "on demand" culture. It requires the patience to systematically gain mastery of a topic or skill.

Because of this, deep work is what will make you the master of your niche.

Deep work is what will set you apart.

DEEP WORK AND CREATIVITY

I've learned (*the hard way*) that it's important for me to identify whether the tasks on my to-do list are knowledge work or deep work, and to schedule my day accordingly.

I have a handful of daily KW tasks that I do early in the day so that they are off my plate

---

[19] http://calnewport.com/blog/2012/11/21/knowledge-workers-are-bad-at-working-and-heres-what-to-do-about-it/

and out of my way. That enables me to set aside the bulk of my time for deep work, the kind of work required to get larger, more significant projects off the ground, through development, and into the refinement and release stages.

My point is this:

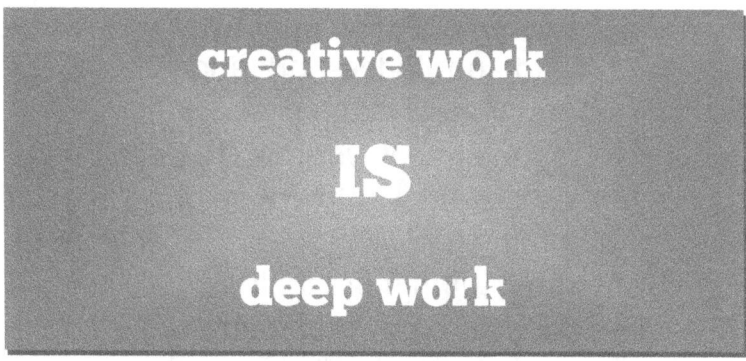

Therefore, creative work requires time. You can't expect to get significant projects done in short bursts throughout the day. That approach doesn't allow you to move from surface, simplistic solutions to truly significant, niche-defining discoveries or contributions.

You've got to put in the time. You've got to do the work. There is no easy. There is no simple.

World-changing contributions require effort, skill, mastery, and clear thinking, and none of that happens in short bursts.

Assignment:

- Consider your typical work day. What percentage of your activity is consumed with knowledge work and what percentage is deep work?
- Is the kind of work you're doing consistent with the type of goals you're aiming for? What needs to change to bring them more in line?
- Jot down your dream ideas. Next to each one, write "KW" or "DW" to indicate what kind of work will primarily be required to accomplish the project with excellence.
- Consider the kind of tempo your life and work will have to maintain in order to see those dreams come to reality.

The present is a present

Julie Coraccio

No matter what your beliefs, there are tools that you can use to help move you forward in your creative life. Here are a few of my favorites.

The Present Moment is A Present

You want to move forward with your creativity, but where are you starting? Most of us are living anywhere but the present moment! We are either:

- Stuck in the past (*I can only be creative if X happens* OR *It never worked for me, so why would it work now?*), or
- Anxious about the future (*What if I never have another creative thought again?*).

The power to change comes in the present moment.

How many of you are focused this very minute on what I am saying? Or are you worried about bills? How you didn't do or say something? Thinking about your next project?

In every moment we can have a fresh start.

I often say that in every moment we have a choice. Doing nothing is also a choice. But we are given a choice in every single moment.

What are you choosing to do?

If you want to be more creative, focus on living in the present moment.

Exercise:

- While doing something physical, notice your thoughts. (I like to do this when I am mowing the lawn, but it could be while washing the dishes, doing laundry, etc.)
- Where are you? Practice bringing your focus back to the present moment and fully embrace and concentrate on the task at hand.

Jim Kukral answers my questions about creativity

 What does your creative spot look like? What is it like when you're flowing and things are just coming and you're creating great things.

I'm a burst worker. I define burst worker as somebody who collects a lot of thoughts in their head for sometimes six months, sometimes three days, sometimes three weeks, but collects the ideas and the concepts of what they want to do in their head, Then just sits down and gets it all done. That's how I work. That's how I prepare projects and websites and membership sites and anything I'm working on.

I kind of formulate it in my head like a guy kneading dough. It's all out there. One day I know I have enough information or I'm ready to go, then I sit down and get it done.

A lot of people don't know people like <u>Einstein</u> was a burst worker the same way. I'm not comparing myself to Einstein. I'm just saying the most famous example I can think of, it was somebody who processed a lot of ideas and thoughts in their head and then once it was all formulated and ready to go they sat down and did that. That's how I function. I just kind of get it all out there when it's all ready to go.

 **That totally makes sense. I guess I'm that way a little bit. Do you have any rituals or practices you go through that help you get in your creative spot when you're ready to sit down and get going?**

No, actually I don't I think the best thing is going back to that motivation thing. The thing that drives me the most is the ability to keep that lifestyle. If I do want to be creative I will play music while I'm trying to work and things like that, but there's no specific rituals or anything I have to do to get it going.

 **Are there any processes that you have for how you evaluate what comes out of those creative times?**

Yeah, obviously the return on investment. If I'm going to spend six months working on a project, what am I going to get out of it the month after and then three years later and five years down the road.

I'm an internet marketing guy, that's my background, so everything ties back to me as if I'm going to spend this much time on something, is it worth my time? That's why you have to track everything. You have to say I spent three months working on this event and I only made a thousand dollars. Guess what? I made minus four cents an hour so that's not a smart business venture. That's how I approach things.

QUICK TIP:

"Creativity is just connecting things. When you ask creative people how they did something, they feel a little guilty because they didn't really do it, they just saw something. It seemed obvious to them after a while. That's because they were able to connect experiences they've had and synthesize new things - From the late

STEVE JOBS

Let others inspire you

Andrea Beltrami

Have you ever had someone tell you a story or confess a struggle to you, and you got inspired or moved by it? Most times your next brilliant idea, article, product or program is just a conversation away. It just takes engaging and stimulating conversations that matter.

The key words there are "that matter"!

Sometimes our creativity is hindered by our inability to get past our self-imposed barriers. We get consumed with our doubts, worries, and the trivial things life throws our way. Often creativity and inspiration pay the price.

When inspiration is fleeting or absent, here's one way you can open the creative flood gates. Shut down the computer, get out of the office/house, and open up a face to face dialogue.

Stop by a friend or family member's house for a visit. Meet a client for coffee or a hike. Look for a local meet-up or enroll in a class or workshop. Go to those places where creative thoughts can flow. You'll be surprised how the engagement and connection will refuel your creativity.

See, others aren't bogged down by your own self-defeating thoughts or burned out by your own internal insecurity loop. They are free to think openly and express their thoughts just because your fears aren't theirs. You may reject their input as silly, but there are kernels of insight to be gleaned. Make no mistake about that!

So the next time your creative tank is empty, don't despair. Instead, give yourself a break, get out of your normal patterns, and refill your tank with meaningful conversations. You'll be refreshed, renewed, and brimming with creativity organically. And hey, have a little fun with great people in the process!

What to do when you "hit the wall

Carey Green

Every one of us has hit the wall. It's that place where your brain shuts down, where the creative juices dry up, where it feels like you're done for the day.

But are you?

I've discovered that's not always the case. Here are a handful of simple things you can try to jump-start yourself when you've come up against brain-lock. Apply what works for you.

- Stop and do some push-ups, sit-ups, jumping-jacks, or any other hyphenated exercise to get your blood pumping. You'll find it not only invigorates your body, but can serve to reset your mind at the same time.

- Take a power-nap (*20 to 30 minutes*)[20]. Sometimes your brain just needs a reboot. It is a biological organ after all. It needs rest from time to time.

- Get something hot/cold to drink (*whatever your pleasure*). Stimulating your sense of taste can serve to stimulate you in other ways.

- Go on a short walk. The diversion and new sensory input can serve to give you a fresh perspective.

- Move to a new location (*outside, inside, to a coffee shop, to the library*). The time it takes to get there and the change of scenery can stimulate new modes of thinking.

- Turn on some music, or turn it off if it's already playing. Change to a different style of music. Again, variety can help you reboot your creative juices.

---

[20] I've been blessed with the ability to fall asleep quickly. My wife said she counted one time after I lay down. 34 seconds. Beat that.

- Breathe deeply. Often, with fresh air comes fresh ideas and perspective.

- Imagine something pleasant. A mental block can produce feelings and attitudes of frustration. Intentionally focusing on things that bring you joy will help to fend off those creativity-suckers and put you back in a positive place.

> **Talk out the issue aloud. Record your rant and listen to it later. Engaging more ways of processing the issue (*verbal included*) can help you see things in a new light.**

- Pray. The humility required to ask God for help can put you in a place where you're able to receive the insights and knowledge you need.

- Go to bed earlier. You may be experiencing the consequences of the fatigue that comes from overwork.

- Get up earlier. It's possible your sleep patterns are not at their optimal point and you are getting too much rest.

- Imagine how a 7-year-old would approach the subject. Imagine how a 90-year-old would approach it. Putting yourself in the shoes of another can help you get beyond the barrier that "self" can be.

- Think of how your favorite movie hero or fictional character would approach the project. Again, getting outside your own head can do wonders.

- Take 5 minutes to work on a crossword puzzle or find-a-word, then return to the project. A different type of mental work can serve as a reset button.

- Stand up (*or sit down*). Or maybe lay down. Changes in posture can be significant ways to give you a new outlook on the situation.

- Take a shower or bath. Go for a quick swim or dip in the pool. These are naturally refreshing and stimulating activities in their own right and can boost your creativity after a long slog.

- Draw or sketch the project visually. Create a mind-map of it. A variety of approaches can stimulate you to see things in a new light.

- Sing... a song you know or something you make up on the spot. Music requires a different form of thinking and a different type of creativity that might help you overcome a hurdle.

- Invert the problem. What would the worst version of what you're creating be like? Consider that thoroughly then flip it back around. The change of perspective can serve you well.

- Introduce the project to someone else and ask for their input or suggestions.

3 simple tips for listening to your creative gut

Katrina Pfannkuch

The creative gut is an interesting creature. It runs on intuition and is a natural part of you. Yet, over time, you might learn or decide not to trust it.

Between crushed expectations, negative experiences with someone close to you, or old patterns you took on from family, your creative gut can lose the upper hand and you don't even realize it. Your inner truth becomes harder to sense and what you really want to see can be hiding behind a super foggy mirror. This makes you feel disconnected from clear inspiration and doubt can start to mess with your focus.

When you run across this bit of confusion it's challenging to know when to release a project, idea, or dream with love, or simply refresh it.

To be sure you are clear and honoring your own creative truth, take a little time to tune-in using one or a few of these simple creative gut-checks:

1. Do you feel one thing in your heart but hear an inner voice in your mind telling you something different?

When the head and heart are in conflict, you have a stand-off. Find a way to calm the mind through meditation, exercise, play, getting out in nature, or just by taking a break. Then wait a few hours or days and check in again.

If you run across the same challenge, there are some unresolved things popping up that require a little more inspection so that your heart and mind can connect instead of oppose each other. It could be an old belief or a desire to hold onto a person or idea that no longer serves you, so be willing to finally release it.

If neither of those seem like a fit, it can simply be an invitation to ask yourself deeper questions about what you really want, not what you've been taught to want. In this case your belief system needs a little refresh so you can become more in tune with what works for the current you.

2. Is there an intriguing idea that cycles back over and over, but you ignore it?

When the same idea makes multiple visits to you, it might be time to look at why you aren't taking action on it. Is there fear in the way? Has someone slashed it down with negative feedback, or is your mind doing a great job of that for you? Are setbacks making the experience more challenging than you expected, so you feel the idea is doomed?

It's extremely easy to think of reasons why you shouldn't or can't do things.

The negatives are much easier to spot because they cause friction and stand out more, even if a hundred awesome things have gone along perfectly.

If a specific idea has a hold on you take some time to reflect and write some notes about it. Jot down why it would be fun or beneficial to pursue or why it might be a disaster. At least that way you've given the creative gut a forum of expression and you can see if still feels like something worth pursuing. Even if the fear seems overwhelming, acknowledging it out loud goes a long way toward soothing it.

3. Are you listening to your inner truth or judging yourself into a corner?

There is a big difference between listening and judging, and it's easy to get them confused. Being objective about your own creativity can be a challenge at times!

To open up some space between what you think you should do and allowing yourself permission to explore a creative direction, it can help to find a person you trust with whom you can talk things over. Or, you can record yourself talking about an idea or sticking point and listen to it a few days later. Saying things out loud and actually hearing your thoughts outside of your mind can create a powerful shift in your point of view.

Another option is to put an idea on ice for a few weeks, then check back with it once you've created clear space. A lot of times the urgency to figure something out pushes you towards judging instead of listening. Space allows you to see if any judgment is clouding the view.

What are some techniques you use to make sure you are tuning into the truth of your creative gut?

Tommy Walker answers my questions about creativity

 **What does the creative spot look like for you?**

It's interesting, because I don't feel particularly "creative" any more. For me, it's more about finding the connections between behaviors, and trying to understand online behavior from a broader perspective (*usually through crunching case studies and academic research*).

This isn't "creative" for me, as much as it is about fitting the pieces together. Once I see it all fall into place, there's is a definitive "A-HA!" moment, but for the most part it's pretty fleeting.

 **Do you have any rituals or practices that help you get into that creative spot?**

Not really. Typically I'm forcing myself to read and think deeply about what it is I'm seeing and how that might relate to that other thing I've read.

If anything, my creative "Zone" looks like <u>Benedict Cumberbatch's</u> <u>Sherlock</u> when he's trying to fit the pieces together on a case. Quite often, if I'm trying to understand an online behavior, I'll imagine the behavior and process through the lens of my personal experiences, conversations I've had with others, case studies I've read, real analytics data etc.

When it works, I'm able to arrive at something that quite often feels bigger than me. That's usually the stuff people who follow my work are really into.

 **What do you do to stay there?**

It's more about having mental fortitude than anything else. I've practiced, intentionally, a lot to build up my own processing power and mental longevity.

I very much view my brain as computer OS, and over the past few years specifically, have been working on upgrading it.

This means working on deep memory techniques so I can mentally pull up research *(which I have organized in a mental file structure that is identical to the one on my computer)*, focusing on complex problems for long periods of time, and analyzing deeply whenever possible.

But for me it's also important to know how to turn that off and thoroughly enjoy myself too. I usually do this by throwing myself into my family and really cutting loose.

 **Do you have a process for how you evaluate what comes out of a creative time?**

Nah. I'm asking myself, "Is it good? And do people seem to like it either by way of comments, shares, or things like that. Is that better than last time?"

My creativity is a product of analysis, so if I can feel that it's good, and if the metrics show that it's good, that's good enough for me.

Though, I'll be honest, I'm also looking for more creative outlets that don't involve so much mental processing. I'm sure that will change once I find that.

 **Are there any beliefs you have about yourself that make you more creative?**

Only that I'm constantly trying to get better, and that I'm realistic with myself that not every day is going to be a "high bar" day.

 **Are there any beliefs you have about yourself that make you less creative?**

Not anymore, no.

Now, I'm trying to take more time for more purely creative pursuits. I am actually looking to find something that I enjoy doing, but am undeniably bad at, like making music or something.

What do you do to fight or minimize those beliefs?

It's about self acceptance for me. I try not to "fight" or "minimize" any negative beliefs but rather embrace that they're part of the process, and they too shall pass.

If something does crop up that doesn't go away, I talk with my wife about it. She is very reassuring and brings me down to earth. She's just as much a part of the process as anything else, and she inspires me more than anything else.

Capture it.

<u>Carey Green</u>

Ideas don't happen on cue or according to a schedule. They come when they come.

In the shower. In a dream. Over a cup of coffee and a conversation with a friend. Driving down the freeway.

What would be the benefit of capturing those ideas while they were still fresh, new, and exciting? Have you ever considered giving it a try?[21]

Throughout history there are many people who have done so, to great benefit. Four of the most famous I've come across are Thomas Edison, Leonardo DiVinci, Marie Curie, and Beatrix Potter.

What I suggest is that you create an "idea journal." I don't know where I first heard of the idea of an idea journal, but having a repository of ideas to draw from for a blog

---

[21] But I won't be responsible for what happens if you do something stupid while driving. Does that qualify as a legal disclaimer?

post, a podcast, an idea for a new info product, or whatever... is a very smart thing to have on hand.

How to start an idea journal

It's really pretty simple to start, but you've got to be intentional about it for it to pay off in the long run.

Some creatives keep a paper note pad and pencil with them at all times. They'll scribble little notes to themselves in the midst of conversations, as they're listening to a symphony performance, or as they're stuck in rush-hour traffic.

> **Remember?**
>
> **Ideas happen when they happen.**

Others log the idea into their smart phone using a voice recognition or productivity app that syncs across all platforms.

It doesn't matter how you do it, the point is that you capture the idea with enough detail so that when you come back to it you'll have a clear idea of what the idea was in the first place.

I can't tell you how many times I've jotted down a "great idea" only to come back to it and not have a clue about what I meant by what I wrote.

Some people re-write the scraps of paper into their journal later on. That way they can have all their ideas in one place. Others drop the voice memo or app file into a computer folder entitled "Ideas."

What do you do with an idea journal?

There are likely as many ways of using an idea journal as there are people who use them.

Some folks wait until they're stuck, or in need of a new blog post, or looking for a new idea for a product or project. They'll pull out their idea journal for inspiration. I've found it to be invaluable in that way.

Others study their idea journal to learn from past mistakes, review the previous day's thoughts, or remind themselves of important tasks they wanted to schedule for attention at a later time. Some of the famous people I mentioned at the beginning of this article did exactly that.

Others make a regular practice of sifting through their scribblings and voice memos to keep them fresh and alive in their minds. Folks who do this often feel that regular review makes their ideas more readily available to them through the course of a given day, simply because they are more "top of mind."

No matter how the ideas are reviewed it's not uncommon for new inspiration, new projects, and world-changing inventions to be the result.

No, that's not an exaggeration.[22]

Some unexpected results.

But there's more benefit to a life journal than just capturing ideas...

You'll become more observant.

---

[22] I NEVER exaggerate!

When you're on the lookout for ideas your awareness of the world and the people around you becomes heightened because you know that ideas come when they come and you want to be ready for them when they do.

You'll develop the ideas more fully.

I've often jotted down an idea and after three or four days I realized that that I'd been developing it in my head almost without effort ever since. By the time I'm ready to work on the idea I've already worked out at least a fundamental outline of how to approach it.

You'll become more motivated.

This happens especially when you jot down a particularly intriguing idea. Something about writing things down makes them more tangible to your subconscious mind. You'll ponder it over and over. You'll become excited to explore it more and begin experimenting with the concepts that swirl around it. You won't have to make yourself pay attention to it because you're already engaged.

What do you think?

How could you use an idea journal to benefit your entrepreneurial journey?

QUICK TIP:

"To live a creative life, we must lose our **fear** of being

WRONG."

from the incredible

Joseph Chilton Pearce

Feel the fear and do it anyway

Julie Coraccio

Our ego stops us from doing so much! The ego will do anything when he or she is afraid: remind you of a failure, keep you focused on why something cannot be done, have you worry about critics, etc.

When I had more of a monkey-mind and was afraid of something, here's what I'd do to "take it down". I'd write out my fear and break it down by asking, "What's the worse that could happen?"

99.99% of what we say in response to that question we can live through and most of those fears never come to pass.

I also ask myself, "Whose voice is that?" Maybe it's society, or a teacher, or parent and not really coming from me!

The first Google Hangouts on Air I ever did, I was nervous because it was new technology for me. Guess what? My biggest fear happened. I hung up on myself! To add insult to injury, someone gave me the big ol' thumbs down on YouTube moments after the HOA was published! I have learned not to care so much what others think. I survived my first Hangout, now I do them weekly, and my You Tube channel continues to grow.

Exercise:

Take a tiny step. Do one small thing that scares you; ask someone out, try a new artistic medium, try a food you have always wanted to, etc. Do something, anything that allows you to feel your fear and move forward.

Tom Rolfson
answers my questions about creativity

 **Tell me what it's like for you when you hit that creative spot or creative flow.**

It's usually a very fast, free-flow of idea exchange with other people. Most often that's where I find myself. I can't turn the camera around but, on the wall directly opposite me right now, is, I think, 20 to 24 post-it notes and there is line after line after line of ideas on there. It's the product of three of us sitting in the room and just jotting ideas down and literally putting it on the wall to see what sticks. So that's one way. How do I define that zone as far as a personal or internal feeling? Probably just one of my most peaceful yet energetic states, if that makes sense.

Do you have any rituals or habits that you put in place to help you get into that place?

In its simplest form, yeah, I rock out. I'm not a musician but I'll pop in some of my favorite music and literally make the walls shake and rock out.

If I'm in that zone, and more often than not, it goes longer than it should because other time constraints or and I fall into a trap of improper self-care. There have been times during a startup of a company where two or three of us have sat down to create for a couple hours and we get on a roll and we find ourselves ordering out for food, and all of the sudden, we're ordering out for food again in five or six hours and just realize that we've been going at it for 10, 12 or more hours. And the following day, you pay the price. You are spent, physically and mentally after doing that but I don't really have to work to maintain that. If I'm in that zone, it can keep going as long as I need.

I think that comes with the entrepreneurial spirit. For many years, I had fun with that joke of, "Start your own business and you can work half days. It means you just don't have a boss to tell you which 12 hours you have to work." During startup of companies, I've worked 6, 7 days weeks - 12 to 18 hours every day. Sitting in the office on the 4th of July while my employees are getting paid and having a good time. I'm doing what I want to do and where I want to be at that time but you have to balance that. You can get too much of it too, depending on your health, relationships and everything else. I do a lot less of that now than I did 20 or 30 years ago.

 **Do you have a process for how you evaluate what comes out of a creative time?**

I think it's a sense of accomplishment when you come out with a product idea or development that you know is worthy of carrying forward and developing further after that session. If we're sitting down and discussing a video concept or a show idea, we can follow many different paths on where we're going to take it. And if at the end of one of those development or writing sessions, we've come out with something concrete with regards to script, that brings the satisfaction that tells me it was successful.

 **Do you see yourself having any mindsets or ways of thinking that help you be creative?**

I believe I have the ability to easily get outside... Think outside of the box. With very little fear of failure or of living in judgment or belief that other people will judge my work.

 **Do you find yourself being protective or reclusive about your ideas or your work?**

Conceptually, no. I will put any idea out there and be willing to accept constructive criticism. I'm not afraid of constructive criticism. I welcome it all.

 **Are there any tips you'd give for getting back into a creative zone once you've come out of it?**

I use meditation on a regular basis. I don't know that I use it specifically to get back into a zone. Sometimes literally just getting away from work, putting the top down on the Corvette, hit the highway and just let the wind in what's left of my hair feel good. That can be a way to reboot, if you will. Reboot or reset. I guess if I find myself in that spot, physically changing things is good; a change of physical location, geographic location. Sometimes I will get out of the studio and just go sit in a coffee shop. It can be buzzing with people and noise and everything else but I'll find myself back in the zone to focusing on what I need. Yeah, it's energy. It's energy that is bouncing off other people.

Act differently

Ryan Healy

Creativity can only flourish when you are reading, thinking, and acting differently than you and other people normally do.

Creative ACTION

leads to creative THOUGHT.

This is why it helps to get out of your routine every now and then.

Drive a different way.

Do things in reverse.

Read books outside the genre or topic of what you'd normally read.

Investigate a new hobby.

Go somewhere you've never gone.

Do something you've never done.

Meet new people and talk with them.

By breaking your routine and doing things that may even be uncomfortable you'll cause your brain to think in new ways. You'll have new thoughts.

And perhaps you can incorporate some of those new thoughts and ideas into your own business activities. Perhaps you'll have a breakthrough.

QUICK TIP:

"Creativity is intelligence **having FUN**."

from the amazing

Albert Einstein

Survival first

Tom Morkes

The best tip I have for anyone who wants to succeed in business is to think about survival first. Not in terms of robustness - surviving setbacks and failures - but in terms of anti-fragility, or actually *benefiting* from setbacks and failures.

Why?

1. Because the startup phase is always tough.
2. Because your first idea won't be the right idea and will require a pivot (*or 100 pivots*).
3. Because you'll hit a rough patch at one point or another.

> **It's these unpredictable events that SINK most startups and most businesses.**

But if you can design your business to not only survive, but benefit from this uncertainty, this unpredictability, this chaos, then success it's just a matter of time.

Hat tip to Nassim Taleb for the ideas mentioned above (*although they are ultimately my best effort to apply his ideas of robustness and anti-fragility to business. I highly recommend the book: Antifragile.*)

Self-care to increase focus and expand creativity

Katrina Pfannkuch

The words "busy entrepreneur", and "self-care" rarely show up in the same sentence. Yet...

> ## self-care is a business owner's MOST IMPORTANT ASSET.

When you feel healthy, clear, and energetic, ideas flow and work moves along easily. You have the stamina and clarity you need to handle clients, manage all the details for your business, and do the big picture visioning to help your business grow in a healthy way. It's also easier to spot and act on an opportunity when you have a clear head and heart.

In order for that to happen, your self-care practice needs to be simple, consistent and a priority in your life, even more so than the work you do.

Here's a simple way to get you out of your head and back into your body so you can reconnect with the energy and clarity you need to manage your day and contribute to your overall health and well-being.

I call this exercise the Big Three. It covers Mind, Body and Spirit - the three essentials for creating mindful balance and a positive self-care practice.

Take a clean sheet of paper and write down the three categories Mind, Body, Spirit. Then make a list of five things or practices that you enjoy in each category.

Next, pick a regular time to practice self-care and add it to your schedule, or make room as you feel out the flow of the day. Pick one item from each of the Big Three categories to practice every day during that time and you have your Mind, Body, Spirit aspects of self-care covered.

This way you can do what you feel drawn to do, keeping things flexible, while also contributing to your overall well-being.

Here are some examples:

Mind:

- meditation
- listening to calming music,
- reading something for pleasure
- journaling
- day dreaming

Body:

- yoga
- healthy cooking
- taking regular desk breaks
- drinking plenty of water
- biking

Spirit:

- connecting with like minds and/or loved ones
- listing things you are grateful for
- quality time with pets and in nature
- regular time alone

- listening to or reading inspirational material

Making room for your mental, physical and spiritual well-being isn't a luxury, it's a necessity. When you make it simple to take care of yourself, you are also much more likely to do it!

Remember, you are the one in charge of your own life - not your clients, family, or friends. While the goal is to do what you love, create your best possible work, and offer great customer service, you need to put self-care first to ensure you have the energy and attitude to pull it all off.

By setting boundaries and creating a simple daily awareness practice of self-care using the Big Three, you empower yourself to be the most innovative, creative and effective in your work and life.

RECOMMENDED CREATIVITY VIDEOS

- Creativity Mind Hacks (1:06:01)

- 29 Ways to Stay Creative (1:05)

- The Creative Life (9:09)

- Creativity is Just Connecting Things (0:47)

- An Ode to Creative Work (1:32)

- Why Man Creates (24:41)

- PressPausePlay (1:21:00)

- Creative Crossroads (10:43)

- Cultures of Creativity (4:30)

- 7 Tips for Creatives (3:24)

RECOMMENDED CREATIVITY PODCASTS

- Accidental Creative Podcast
- How Clutter Kills Your Creativity (an Interview with Jeff Goins)
- How Creativity Works (interview with Jonah Lehrer)
- Uncanny Creativity Podcast
- Episode #96 of Less Doing, More Living (Interview with Michael Gelb)
- Maya Angelou on Courage and Creativity
- Do The Things That Scare You
- Teaching Creativity
- The Source of Creativity

- [Creating Creativity: Success Outside the Box](#) (Pat Flynn)

Let me introduce you to the great folks who contributed to this incredible book.

ANDREA BELTRAMI

As I've poked around Dre's website and interacted with her in various social media platforms I've come to learn a couple of things about her.

Dre loves life and she has a heart to help people. I really like that.

She's into branding, design, and all kinds of great looking stuff. You can see her portfolio here - http://thebrandedsolopreneur.com/portfolio/.

If you want to check out more of Dre's stuff or connect with her, you can do that at her site http://www.TheBrandedSolopreneur.com

DONNIE BRYANT

DB is a guy who does great work in marketing and copyrighting. He's not your typical marketer or marketing consultant, either.

And on his website DB brags that he intends to be the most generous guy you know. If you're looking for some help with your marketing or need some copyrighting work, you should put that statement to the test.

DB also does a lot of work with local businesses in the Chicagoland area. So if you're there, so is he. You should connect.

You can reach out to DB through his website http://www.Donnie-Bryant.com

STEPHANIE CALAHAN

Out of all the people featured in this book, Stephanie is one that I've known the longest, and we've never even met in person.

I met Stephanie through the Christians in Business community on Google Plus and found out pretty quickly that she's a gem.

You talk about enthusiasm, energy, and desire to live life positively and powerfully - you've just described Stephanie.

Stephanie is a business coach and consultant, working with people of all stripes - entrepreneurs, coaches, consultants, authors, speakers - you name it.

From what I've seen, Stephanie knows here stuff and can probably help you with yours.

Find Stephanie at her website www.StephanieCalahan.com

JULIE CORACCIO

As I've gotten to know Julie a bit I've found her to be a very eager and energetic person. Every email I've received from her has been laced with encouragement.

Julie a professional organizer and writer, and serves as an individual and group coach as well. She loves to help people lead a more joyful and fulfilling life.

She has a podcast "Clearing Away the Clutter" and Youtube channel which you might enjoy checking out.

Find Julie through her website at www.ReawakenYourBrilliance.com

DAN CRASK

Dan's a guy I got to know pretty early in my online exploits. I don't think I could say enough about this man. He's honest, dependable, and very, very good at what he does.

Dan is the "Brand Shepherd" specializing in helping businesses discover their brand identity and put together a plan to get their new identity into the marketplace. His company, "Brand Shepherd" specializes in creative direction, project management, branding, and though leadership.

You can connect with Dan through his website:
www.BrandShepherd.com

RICK ELIASON

As you can tell from his picture, Rick's a lot of fun.. .and he's an SEO expert who is very generous in the resources he produces and gives away. I first came across Rick on Google Plus and have been very impressed with the amount of stuff he cranks out.

He's especially good at conversion optimization, social media marketing, and Google Plus.

You can connect with Rick at www.RickEliason.com

SUSAN FINCH

Susan. What can I say about Susan?

She's been in business since 2001 and has loved it ever since.

She works with clients on their social media strategy, writing, and management, and has recently become a "wingman" for podcasts and live on-air events. That includes providing all the graphics for the event, testing, launching, recapping through writings and annotations, and repurposing the event for use in other ways. social media campaigns and content strategies

Wow!

Connect with Susan at www.SusanFinch.com

CAREY GREEN

It's my turn. I do lots of things in life, but in terms of business all of my ventures are one the internet. I teach people how to build streams of side-income revenue to supplement their existing income or build a business that can take over and surpass their current income altogether. I do so through coaching, mini-courses, writing, and sharing the insights I've learned through my own entrepreneurial adventures. That includes email marketing, course creation, outsourcing, business systematization, habit formation, and more. You can see all about that at http://www.SideIncomeAcademy.com.

I also run a growing podcast production service and write books (see the back of this book). You can contact me atwww.CareyGreen.com

RYAN M. HEALY

Ryan is a direct response copywriter. But from what I've learned that's an understatement.

Ryan is the most referred direct response copywriter on the internet. He writes sales letters and emails, and has discovered what really works to bring in new customers and bigger profits. Since 2002, he's worked with 150+ clients, including major financial publishers like Agora Financial, Lombardi Publishing, Dent Research, and Contrarian Profits. And he's also worked with well-known marketing experts like Alex Mandossian, Terry Dean, and Josh Bezoni.

Ryan has also done quality control on tens of thousands of PPC ads for dozens of major companies, including Pottery Barn Kids, GEICO, Dell, Vitamin Shoppe, 1800PetMeds.com, KAYAK, Angie's List, ADT, Iberostar, Zazzle, and Ask.com.

Visit Ryan online at www.RyanHealy.com

PHYLLIS KHARE

If you spend any time in the business communities of the social media platforms, you've probably heard of Phyllis.

Phyllis is Co-founder of www.SocialMediaManagerSchool.com, Founder of TimeBliss.ME and author of Social Media eLearning Kit for Dummies and co-author of Facebook Marketing All-In-One for Dummies,. Senior Content Editor for www.MyPath101.com and Adjunct Instructor at www.MUM.edu .

She has learned how to be a great social media manager with all different types of entrepreneurs and is full of stories and adventures in teaching and training these high-powered people.

She's a member of Best Keynote Speakers and has written and presented for some of the largest social media blogs and events like Social Media Examiner and Marketing Profs.

Connect with Phyllis at www.PhyllisKhare.com

JIM KUKRAL

Jim is a no nonsense, lifestyle business entrepreneur. He does what he does to be a benefit to people and create the lifestyle he wants for himself and his family.

For over 16-years, Jim Kukral has helped small businesses and large companies like Fedex, Sherwin Williams, Ernst & Young and Progressive Auto Insurance understand how to build up their online business presence and leverage social media.

He's an innovator, author, podcaster, and was recently named one of "The Most Influential Small Business People on Twitter" according to Dun & Bradstreet.

Connect with Jim at www.JimKukral.com

DANIEL J. LEWIS

Daniel is a great guy who really knows his stuff.

He's an award-winning podcaster who helps others launch and improve their own podcasts for sharing their passions and finding success.

Daniel creates training resources and podcasting tools (like My Podcast Reviews); offers one-on-one consulting; speaks on social media and podcasting, and hosts a network of award-nominated shows covering how to podcast, clean-comedy, and the #1 unofficial podcast for ABC's hit drama "Once Upon a Time."

Connect with Daniel at www.DanielJLewis.net

TOM MORKES

The first thing I want to say about Tom is that he's a Veteran of the U.S. military. He graduated from The United States Military Academy at West Point and spent 5 years active duty as a commissioned officer in the U.S. Army.

Thanks for your service, Tom.

Tom is the CEO of Insurgent Publishing, a boutique publishing company that makes books for the creative outliers of the world. Tom is the author of four books, which you can find here.

ITom co-founded and launched The Flight Formula, the worlds first ever heart-centered incubator. He's also co-founded High Speed Low Drag alongside John Lee Dumas and Antonio Centeno.

Connect with Tom at www.TomMorkes.com

KATRINA PFANNKUCH

Katrina is a very sweet gal who's given generously to this project.

She's a creativity consultant, writer, intuitive, empath, and reiki master. She helps people move past their creative and mental bloks to become more clear, focused, and expressive in their business or creative work.

She also speaks and writes about creativity, mindfulness, self-care, entrepreneurship and a variety of topics related to personal development.

Connect with Katrina at www.creativekatrina.com

TOM
ROLFSON

Tom is one of the guys I was able to connect with via video. I was amazed to see how long we'd been on the call. Tom was great to connect with.

Tom's a serial entrepreneur, investor, producer, and marketer. He's one of the first to dive in to ideas that others only talk about.

I guess you could say Tom is an innovator. He pioneered taking the first bulletin board technology and putting it into commercial use. He's worked with the U.S. Secret Service, created social media networks, created the first systems to sell concert tickets online, and has created and sold dot com businesses.

Tom's a wealth of knowledge and a generous man.

The best place to connect with Tom is on Google+ -
https://plus.google.com/+TomRolfson

MARTIN SHERVINGTON

Martin is an all-around great guy. He's a Google+ whiz and runs a number of communities and businesses that focus on helping businesses maximize their presence and impact through the G+ platorm.

Martin's got degrees in law, business, and organizational psychology and is a Master Practitioner NLP. He's spent almost 20 years working as an executive coach, business consultant and marketing psychologist.

Connect with Martin at www.MartinShervington.com

TOMMY
WALKER

Tommy is one of the bigwhigs over at the well-known internet site www.Shopify.com. where he serves businesses in optimizing their websites for optimal sales conversions.

Tommy's also the host of "Inside the Mind" a fresh new show about Online Marketing Strategy.

Connect with Tommy through is Google Plus profile-https://plus.google.com/u/0/+TommyWalker1/about

Don't miss BOOK TWO...

Get your copy now!

www.CareyGreen.com/MindHacks

More books by this author

RECHARGE: Devotional bible study methods to recharge your spiritual growth, improve your spiritual health,& grow your intimacy with God.

www.CareyGreen.com/books

The Marriage Improvement Project Apply the principles in this book and watch God transform your marriage forever! The MIP is designed for spouses to complete separately with team projects to work on periodically together.
www.CareyGreen.com/books

Moving Toward God: Finding God from square one: A newbie's guide to the basics of Christianity: 19 lessons for spiritual growth

www.CareyGreen.com/books

The Elder Training Handbook: This is a guide for identifying and equipping men for the role of church Elder, and is powerfully practical... from assessment to evaluation to installation.
www.CareyGreen.com/books

Fiction Releases

Dragon Slayer: Beginnings: Book One in the Dragon Slayer Chronicles. A coming of age story that follows a young boy, snatched from his home by a vicious dragon and set on a path to becoming the leader of an unlikely band of dragon slayers.
www.CareyGreen.com/books

Dragon Slayer: Rising: Book Two in the Dragon Slayer Chronicles. The Dragon Masters rise, taking the lands by storm. Hon and his friends rise up to meet the challenge, but can they overcome such powerful and crafty opponents?
www.CareyGreen.com/books

****